Alfred Te

The Foresters

Robin Hood and Maid Marian

Elibron Classics
www.elibron.com

Elibron Classics series.

© 2007 Adamant Media Corporation.

ISBN 1-4021-4710-4 (paperback)
ISBN 1-4212-7628-3 (hardcover)

This Elibron Classics Replica Edition is an unabridged facsimile
of the edition published in 1892 by Macmillan and Co., London, New Yo

ROBIN HOOD

AND

MAID MARIAN

THE FORESTERS

ROBIN HOOD AND MAID MARIAN

BY

ALFRED

LORD TENNYSON

POET LAUREATE

London

MACMILLAN AND CO.

AND NEW YORK

1892

DRAMATIS PERSONÆ.

ROBIN HOOD, *Earl of Huntingdon.*
KING RICHARD, *Cœur de Lion.*
PRINCE JOHN.
LITTLE JOHN,
WILL SCARLET,
FRIAR TUCK, *Followers of Robin Hood.*
MUCH,
A JUSTICIARY.
SHERIFF OF NOTTINGHAM.
ABBOT OF ST. MARY'S.
SIR RICHARD LEA.
WALTER LEA, *son of Sir Richard Lea.*
MAID MARIAN, *daughter of Sir Richard Lea.*
KATE, *attendant on Marian.*
OLD WOMAN.

Retainers, Messengers, Merry Men, Mercenaries, Friars, Beggars, Sailors, Peasants (men and women), &c.

ACT I

SCENE I

THE BOND

SCENES II, III

THE OUTLAWRY

THE FORESTERS

ACT I

Kate (*gathering flowers*).

These roses for my Lady Marian; these lilies to lighten Sir Richard's black room, where he sits and eats his heart for want of money to pay the Abbot.

[*Sings.*

The warrior Earl of Allendale,
He loved the Lady Anne;
The lady loved the master well,
The maid she loved the man.

All in the castle garden,
Or ever the day began,
The lady gave a rose to the Earl,
The maid a rose to the man.

𝔈   B

' I go to fight in Scotland
  With many a savage clan;'
The lady gave her hand to the Earl,
  The maid her hand to the man.

' Farewell, farewell, my warrior Earl!'
  And ever a tear down ran.
She gave a weeping kiss to the Earl,
  And the maid a kiss to the man.

Enter four ragged RETAINERS.

FIRST RETAINER.

You do well, Mistress Kate, to sing and to gather roses.   You be fed with tit-bits, you, and we be dogs that have only the bones, till we be only bones our own selves.

SECOND RETAINER.

I am fed with tit-bits no more than you are, but I keep a good heart and make the most of it, and, truth to say, Sir Richard and my Lady Marian fare wellnigh as sparely as their people.

THIRD RETAINER.

And look at our suits, out at knee, out at elbow. We be more like scarecrows in a field than decent serving men; and then, I pray you, look at Robin Earl of Huntingdon's men.

First Retainer.

She hath looked well at one of 'em, Little John.

Third Retainer.

Ay, how fine they be in their liveries, and each of 'em as full of meat as an egg, and as sleek and as round-about as a mellow codlin.

Fourth Retainer.

But I be worse off than any of you, for I be lean by nature, and if you cram me crop-full I be little better than Famine in the picture, but if you starve me I be Gaffer Death himself. I would like to show you, Mistress Kate, how bare and spare I be on the rib : I be lanker than an old horse turned out to die on the common.

Kate.

Spare me thy spare ribs, I pray thee ; but now I ask you all, did none of you love young Walter Lea ?

First Retainer.

Ay, if he had not gone to fight the king's battles, we should have better battels at home.

Kate.

Right as an Oxford scholar, but the boy was taken prisoner by the Moors.

FIRST RETAINER.

Ay.

KATE.

And Sir Richard was told he might be ransomed for two thousand marks in gold.

FIRST RETAINER.

Ay.

KATE.

Then he borrowed the monies from the Abbot of York, the Sheriff's brother. And if they be not paid back at the end of the year, the land goes to the Abbot.

FIRST RETAINER.

No news of young Walter?

KATE.

None, nor of the gold, nor the man who took out the gold: but now ye know why we live so stintedly, and why ye have so few grains to peck at. Sir Richard must scrape and scrape till he get to the land again. Come, come, why do ye loiter here? Carry fresh rushes into the dining-hall, for those that are there they be so greasy and smell so vilely that my Lady Marian holds her nose when she steps across it.

FOURTH RETAINER.

Why there, now! that very word 'greasy' hath a kind of unction in it, a smack of relish about it. The rats have gnawed 'em already. I pray Heaven we may not have to take to the rushes.   [*Exeunt.*

KATE.

Poor fellows!

The lady gave her hand to the Earl,
The maid her hand to the man.

Enter LITTLE JOHN.

LITTLE JOHN.

My master, Robin the Earl, is always a-telling us that every man, for the sake of the great blessed Mother in heaven, and for the love of his own little mother on earth, should handle all womankind gently, and hold them in all honour, and speak small to 'em, and not scare 'em, but go about to come at their love with all manner of homages, and observances, and circumbendibuses.

KATE.

The lady gave a rose to the Earl,
The maid a rose to the man.

LITTLE JOHN (*seeing her*).

O the sacred little thing! What a shape! what lovely arms! A rose to the man! Ay, the man had given her a rose and she gave him another.

KATE.

Shall I keep one little rose for Little John? No.

LITTLE JOHN.

There, there! You see I was right. She hath a tenderness toward me, but is too shy to show it. It is in her, in the woman, and the man must bring it out of her.

KATE.

She gave a weeping kiss to the Earl,
The maid a kiss to the man.

LITTLE JOHN.

Did she? But there I am sure the ballad is at fault. It should have told us how the man first kissed the maid. She doesn't see me. Shall I be bold? shall I touch her? shall I give her the first kiss? O sweet Kate, my first love, the first kiss, the first kiss!

KATE (*turns and kisses him*).

Why lookest thou so amazed?

LITTLE JOHN.

I cannot tell; but I came to give thee the first kiss, and thou hast given it me.

KATE.

But if a man and a maid care for one another, does it matter so much if the maid give the first kiss?

LITTLE JOHN.

I cannot tell, but I had sooner have given thee the first kiss. I was dreaming of it all the way hither.

KATE.

Dream of it, then, all the way back, for now I will have none of it.

LITTLE JOHN.

Nay, now thou hast given me the man's kiss, let me give thee the maid's.

KATE.

If thou draw one inch nearer, I will give thee a buffet on the face.

LITTLE JOHN.

Wilt thou not give me rather the little rose for Little John?

Kate (*throws it down and tramples on it*).

There !

[Kate, *seeing* Marian, *exit hurriedly.*

Enter Marian (*singing*).

Love flew in at the window
    As Wealth walk'd in at the door.
'You have come for you saw Wealth coming,' said I.
But he flutter'd his wings with a sweet little cry,
    I'll cleave to you rich or poor.

Wealth dropt out of the window,
    Poverty crept thro' the door.
' Well now you would fain follow Wealth,' said I,
But he flutter'd his wings as he gave me the lie,
    I cling to you all the more.

Little John.

Thanks, my lady—inasmuch as I am a true believer in true love myself, and your Ladyship hath sung the old proverb out of fashion.

Marian.

Ay but thou hast ruffled my woman, Little John. She hath the fire in her face and the dew in her eyes. I believed thee to be too solemn and formal to be a ruffler. Out upon thee !

LITTLE JOHN.

I am no ruffler, my lady ; but I pray you, my lady,
if a man and a maid love one another, may the maid
give the first kiss?

MARIAN.

It will be all the more gracious of her if she do.

LITTLE JOHN.

I cannot tell.   Manners be so corrupt, and these
are the days of Prince John.   [*Exit.*

Enter SIR RICHARD LEA (*reading a bond*).

SIR RICHARD.

Marian !

MARIAN.

Father !

SIR RICHARD.

Who parted from thee even now ?

MARIAN.

That strange starched stiff creature, Little John,
the Earl's man.   He would grapple with a lion like
the King, and is flustered by a girl's kiss.

SIR RICHARD.

There never was an Earl so true a friend of the people as Lord Robin of Huntingdon.

MARIAN.

A gallant Earl. I love him as I hate John.

SIR RICHARD.

I fear me he hath wasted his revenues in the service of our good king Richard against the party of John, as I have done, as I have done: and where is Richard?

MARIAN.

Cleave to him, father! he will come home at last.

SIR RICHARD.

I trust he will, but if he do not I and thou are but beggars.

MARIAN.

We will be beggar'd then and be true to the King.

SIR RICHARD.

Thou speakest like a fool or a woman. Canst thou endure to be a beggar whose whole life hath been folded like a blossom in the sheath, like a careless sleeper in the down ; who never hast felt a want, to whom all things, up to this present, have come as freely as heaven's air and mother's milk ?

MARIAN.

Tut, father ! I am none of your delicate Norman maidens who can only broider and mayhap ride a-hawking with the help of the men.   I can bake and I can brew, and by all the saints I can shoot almost as closely with the bow as the great Earl himself. I have played at the foils too with Kate : but is not to-day his birthday ?

SIR RICHARD.

Dost thou love him indeed, that thou keepest a record of his birthdays ?   Thou knowest that the Sheriff of Nottingham loves thee.

MARIAN.

The Sheriff dare to love me ? me who worship Robin the great Earl of Huntingdon ?   I love him as a damsel of his day might have loved Harold the Saxon, or Hereward the Wake.   They both fought against the tyranny of the kings, the Normans.   But then your Sheriff, your little man, if he dare to fight at all, would fight for his rents, his leases, his houses, his monies, his oxen, his dinners, himself. Now your great man, your Robin, all England's Robin, fights not for himself but for the people of England. This John—this Norman tyranny—the stream is bearing us all down, and our little Sheriff will ever swim with the stream! but our great man, our Robin, against it. And how often in old histories have the great men striven against the stream, and how often in the long sweep of years to come must the great man strive against it again to save his country, and the liberties of his people! God bless our well-beloved Robin, Earl of Huntingdon.

Sir Richard.

Ay, ay. He wore thy colours once at a tourney. I am old and forget. Was Prince John there?

Marian.

The Sheriff of Nottingham was there—not John.

Sir Richard.

Beware of John and the Sheriff of Nottingham. They hunt in couples, and when they look at a maid they blast her.

Marian.

Then the maid is not high-hearted enough.

Sir Richard.

There—there—be not a fool again. Their aim is ever at that which flies highest—but O girl, girl, I am almost in despair. Those two thousand marks lent me by the Abbot for the ransom of my son Walter—I believed this Abbot of the party of King Richard, and he hath sold himself to that beast John —they must be paid in a year and a month, or I lose the land. There is one that should be grateful to me overseas, a Count in Brittany—he lives near Quimper. I saved his life once in battle. He has monies. I will go to him. I saved him. I will try him. I am all but sure of him. I will go to him.

Marian.

And I will follow thee, and God help us both.

Sir Richard.

Child, thou shouldst marry one who will pay the mortgage. This Robin, this Earl of Huntingdon— he is a friend of Richard—I know not, but he may save the land, he may save the land.

Marian (*showing a cross hung round her neck*).

Father, you see this cross?

SIR RICHARD.

Ay the King, thy godfather, gave it thee when a baby.

MARIAN.

And he said that whenever I married he would give me away, and on this cross I have sworn [*kisses it*] that till I myself pass away, there is no other man that shall give me away.

SIR RICHARD.

Lo there——thou art fool again——I am all as loyal as thyself, but what a vow! what a vow!

Re-enter LITTLE JOHN.

LITTLE JOHN.

My Lady Marian, your woman so flustered me that I forgot my message from the Earl. To-day he hath accomplished his thirtieth birthday, and he prays your ladyship and your ladyship's father to be present at his banquet to-night.

MARIAN.
Say, we will come.

LITTLE JOHN.

And I pray you, my lady, to stand between me and your woman, Kate.

MARIAN.

I will speak with her.

LITTLE JOHN.

I thank you, my lady, and I wish you and your ladyship's father a most exceedingly good morning.

[*Exit.*

SIR RICHARD.

Thou hast answered for me, but I know not if I will let thee go.

MARIAN.

I mean to go.

SIR RICHARD.

Not if I barred thee up in thy chamber, like a bird in a cage.

MARIAN.

Then I would drop from the casement, like a spider.

SIR RICHARD.

But I would hoist the drawbridge, like thy master.

MARIAN.

And I would swim the moat, like an otter.

SIR RICHARD.

But I would set my men-at-arms to oppose thee, like the Lord of the Castle.

MARIAN.

And I would break through them all, like the King of England.

SIR RICHARD.

Well, thou shalt go, but O the land! the land! my great great great grandfather, my great great grandfather, my great grandfather, my grandfather and my own father—they were born and bred on it —it was their mother—they have trodden it for half a thousand years, and whenever I set my own foot on it I say to it, Thou art mine, and it answers, I am thine to the very heart of the earth—but now I have lost my gold, I have lost my son, and I shall lose my land also.   Down to the devil with this bond that beggars me !   [*Flings down the bond.*

MARIAN.

Take it again, dear father, be not wroth at the dumb parchment. Sufficient for the day, dear father ! let us be merry to-night at the banquet.

SCENE II.—*A hall in the house of* ROBIN HOOD *the Earl of Huntingdon.   Doors open into a banqueting-hall where he is at feast with his friends.*

DRINKING SONG.

Long live Richard,
  Robin and Richard !
Long live Richard !
  Down with John !
Drink to the Lion-heart
  Every one !
Pledge the Plantagenet,
  Him that is gone.
Who knows whither ?
  God's good Angel
Help him back hither,
  And down with John !
Long live Robin,
  Robin and Richard !
Long live Robin,
  And down with John !

Enter PRINCE JOHN *disguised as a monk and the* SHERIFF OF NOTTINGHAM.   *Cries of* ' *Down with John,*' ' *Long live King Richard,*' ' *Down with John.*'

C

PRINCE JOHN.

Down with John! ha.   Shall I be known? is my disguise perfect?

SHERIFF.

Perfect—who should know you for Prince John, so that you keep the cowl down and speak not?

[*Shouts from the banquet-room.*

PRINCE JOHN.

Thou and I will still these revelries presently.

[*Shouts,* 'Long live King Richard!'

I come here to see this daughter of Sir Richard of the Lea and if her beauties answer their report.   If so—

SHERIFF.

If so—   [*Shouts,* 'Down with John!'

PRINCE JOHN.

You hear!

SHERIFF.

Yes, my lord, fear not.   I will answer for you.

Enter LITTLE JOHN, SCARLET, MUCH, *&c., from the banquet singing a snatch of the Drinking Song.*

LITTLE JOHN.

I am a silent man myself, and all the more wonder
at our Earl.   What a wealth of words—O Lord, I
will live and die for King Richard—not so much for
the cause as for the Earl.   O Lord, I am easily led
by words, but I think the Earl hath right.   Scarlet,
hath not the Earl right?   What makes thee so down
in the mouth?

SCARLET.

I doubt not, I doubt not, and though I be down
in the mouth, I will swear by the head of the Earl.

LITTLE JOHN.

Thou Much, miller's son, hath not the Earl right?

MUCH.

More water goes by the mill than the miller wots
of, and more goes to make right than I know of, but
for all that I will swear the Earl hath right.   But they
are coming hither for the dance—

Enter FRIAR TUCK.

be they not, Friar Tuck?   Thou art the Earl's con-
fessor and shouldst know.

TUCK.

Ay, ay, and but that I am a man of weight, and the weight of the church to boot on my shoulders, I would dance too.   Fa, la, la, fa, la, la.   [*Capering.*

MUCH.

But doth not the weight of the flesh at odd times overbalance the weight of the church, ha friar?

TUCK.

Homo sum.   I love my dinner—but I can fast, I can fast ; and as to other frailties of the flesh—out upon thee! Homo sum, sed virgo sum, I am a virgin, my masters, I am a virgin.

MUCH.

And a virgin, my masters, three yards about the waist is like to remain a virgin, for who could embrace such an armful of joy?

TUCK.

Knave, there is a lot of wild fellows in Sherwood Forest who hold by King Richard.   If ever I meet thee there, I will break thy sconce with my quarter-staff.

Enter from the banqueting-hall SIR RICHARD LEA, ROBIN HOOD, *&c.*

ROBIN.

My guests and friends, Sir Richard, all of you
Who deign to honour this my thirtieth year,
And some of you were prophets that I might be
Now that the sun our King is gone, the light
Of these dark hours; but this new moon, I fear,
Is darkness.   Nay, this may be the last time
When I shall hold my birthday in this hall:
I may be outlaw'd, I have heard a rumour.

ALL.

God forbid!

ROBIN.

Nay, but we have no news of Richard yet,
And ye did wrong in crying 'Down with John;'
For be he dead, then John may be our King.

ALL.

God forbid!

ROBIN.

Ay God forbid,
But if it be so we must bear with John.

The man is able enough——no lack of wit,
And apt at arms and shrewd in policy.
Courteous enough too when he wills; and yet
I hate him for his want of chivalry.
He that can pluck the flower of maidenhood
From off the stalk and trample it in the mire,
And boast that he hath trampled it.　I hate him,
I hate the man.　I may not hate the King
For aught I know,
So that our Barons bring his baseness under.
I think they will be mightier than the king.

　　　　　　　　　　　　　　　　[*Dance music.*

(MARIAN *enters with other damsels.*)

ROBIN.

The high Heaven guard thee from his wantonness,
Who art the fairest flower of maidenhood
That ever blossom'd on this English isle.

MARIAN.

Cloud not thy birthday with one fear for me.
My lord, myself and my good father pray
Thy thirtieth summer may be thirty-fold
As happy as any of those that went before.

ROBIN.

My Lady Marian you can make it so
If you will deign to tread a measure with me.

MARIAN.

Full willingly, my lord.

[*They dance.*

ROBIN (*after dance*).

My Lady, will you answer me a question?

MARIAN.

Any that you may ask.

ROBIN.

A question that every true man asks of a woman
once in his life.

MARIAN.

I will not answer it, my lord, till King Richard
come home again.

PRINCE JOHN (*to* SHERIFF).

How she looks up at him, how she holds her face!
Now if she kiss him, I will have his head.

SHERIFF.

Peace, my lord; the Earl and Sir Richard come this way.

ROBIN.

Must you have these monies before the year and the month end?

SIR RICHARD.

Or I forfeit my land to the Abbot.   I must pass overseas to one that I trust will help me.

ROBIN.

Leaving your fair Marian alone here.

SIR RICHARD.

Ay, for she hath somewhat of the lioness in her, and there be men-at-arms to guard her.

[ROBIN, SIR RICHARD, *and* MARIAN *pass on.*

PRINCE JOHN (*to* SHERIFF).

Why that will be our opportunity
When I and thou will rob the nest of her.

SHERIFF.

Good Prince, art thou in need of any gold?

PRINCE JOHN.

Gold? why? not now.

SHERIFF.

I would give thee any gold
So that myself alone might rob the nest.

PRINCE JOHN.

Well, well then, thou shalt rob the nest alone.

SHERIFF.

Swear to me by that relic on thy neck.

PRINCE JOHN.

I swear then by this relic on my neck—
No, no, I will not swear by this; I keep it
For holy vows made to the blessed Saints
Not pleasures, women's matters.
Dost thou mistrust me? Am I not thy friend?
Beware, man, lest thou lose thy faith in me.
I love thee much; and as I *am* thy friend,
I promise thee to make this Marian thine.
Go now and ask the maid to dance with thee,
And learn from her if she do love this Earl.

SHERIFF (*advancing toward* MARIAN *and* ROBIN).

Pretty mistress!

ROBIN.

What art thou, man?   Sheriff of Nottingham?

SHERIFF.

Ay, my lord.   I and my friend, this monk, were
here belated, and seeing the hospitable lights in your
castle, and knowing the fame of your hospitality, we
ventured in uninvited.

ROBIN.

You are welcome, though I fear you be of those
who hold more by John than Richard.

SHERIFF.

True, for through John I had my sheriffship.   I
am John's till Richard come back again, and then I
am Richard's.   Pretty mistress, will you dance?

[*They dance.*

ROBIN (*talking to* PRINCE JOHN).

What monk of what convent art thou?   Why
wearest thou thy cowl to hide thy face?

[PRINCE JOHN *shakes his head.*

Is he deaf, or dumb, or daft, or drunk belike?

[PRINCE JOHN *shakes his head.*

Why comest thou like a death's head at my feast?

> [PRINCE JOHN *points to the* SHERIFF,
> *who is dancing with* MARIAN.

Is he thy mouthpiece, thine interpreter?

> [PRINCE JOHN *nods.*

SHERIFF (*to* MARIAN *as they pass*).

Beware of John!

MARIAN.

I hate him.

SHERIFF.

> Would you cast

An eye of favour on me, I would pay
My brother all his debt and save the land.

MARIAN.

I cannot answer thee till Richard come.

SHERIFF.

And when he comes?

MARIAN.

> Well, you must wait till then.

LITTLE JOHN (*dancing with* KATE).

Is it made up?   Will you kiss me?

KATE.

You shall give me the first kiss.

LITTLE JOHN.

There (*kisses her*).   Now thine.

KATE.

You shall wait for mine till Sir Richard has paid
the Abbot.   [*They pass on.*

[*The* SHERIFF *leaves* MARIAN *with her father
and comes toward* ROBIN.

ROBIN (*to* SHERIFF, PRINCE JOHN *standing by*).

Sheriff, thy friend, this monk, is but a statue.

SHERIFF.

Pardon him, my lord : he is a holy Palmer, bounden
by a vow not to show his face, nor to speak word to
anyone, till he join King Richard in the Holy Land.

ROBIN.

Going to the Holy Land to Richard ! Give me
thy hand and tell him —— Why, what a cold grasp
is thine—as if thou didst repent thy courtesy even in
the doing it.   That is no true man's hand.   I hate
hidden faces.

SHERIFF.

Pardon him again, I pray you ; but the twilight
of the coming day already glimmers in the east.   We
thank you, and farewell.

ROBIN.

Farewell, farewell.   I hate hidden faces.
                    [*Exeunt* PRINCE JOHN *and* SHERIFF.

SIR RICHARD (*coming forward with* MAID MARIAN).

How close the Sheriff peer'd into thine eyes !
What did he say to thee ?

MARIAN.

                    Bade me beware
Of John : what maid but would beware of John ?

SIR RICHARD.

What else ?

MARIAN.

I care not what he said.

SIR RICHARD.

                              What else ?

MARIAN.

That if I cast an eye of favour on him,
Himself would pay this mortgage to his brother,
And save the land.

SIR RICHARD.

Did he say so, the Sheriff?

ROBIN.

I fear this Abbot is a heart of flint,
Hard as the stones of his abbey.
O good Sir Richard,
I am sorry my exchequer runs so low
I cannot help you in this exigency;
For though my men and I flash out at times
Of festival like burnish'd summer-flies,
We make but one hour's buzz, are only like
The rainbow of a momentary sun.
I am mortgaged as thyself.

SIR RICHARD.

Ay! I warrant thee—thou canst not be sorrier than
I am. Come away, daughter.

ROBIN.

Farewell, Sir Richard; farewell, sweet Marian.

MARIAN.

Till better times.

ROBIN.

But if the better times should never come?

MARIAN.

Then I shall be no worse.

ROBIN.

And if the worst time come?

MARIAN.

Why then I will be better than the time.

ROBIN.

This ring my mother gave me: it was her own
Betrothal ring. She pray'd me when I loved
A maid with all my heart to pass it down
A finger of that hand which should be mine
Thereafter. Will you have it? Will you wear it?

MARIAN.

Ay, noble Earl, and never part with it.

SIR RICHARD LEA (*coming up*).

Not till she clean forget thee, noble Earl.

MARIAN.

Forget *him*——never——by this Holy Cross
Which good King Richard gave me when a child—
Never!

Not while the swallow skims along the ground,
And while the lark flies up and touches heaven !
Not while the smoke floats from the cottage roof,
And the white cloud is roll'd along the sky !
Not while the rivulet babbles by the door,
And the great breaker beats upon the beach !
Never—
Till Nature, high and low, and great and small
Forgets herself, and all her loves and hates
Sink again into chaos.

SIR RICHARD LEA.

Away ! away !

[*Exeunt to music.*

SCENE III.—*Same as Scene II.*

ROBIN *and his men.*

ROBIN.

All gone !—my ring—I am happy—should be happy.
She took my ring.   I trust she loves me—yet
I heard this Sheriff tell her he would pay
The mortgage if she favour'd him.   I fear
Not her, the father's power upon her.

Friends, (*to his men*)

I am only merry for an hour or two

Upon a birthday : if this life of ours
Be a good glad thing, why should we make us merry
Because a year of it is gone? but Hope
Smiles from the threshold of the year to come
Whispering 'it will be happier,' and old faces
Press round us, and warm hands close with warm
        hands,
And thro' the blood the wine leaps to the brain
Like April sap to the topmost tree, that shoots
New buds to heaven, whereon the throstle rock'd
Sings a new song to the new year—and you
Strike up a song, my friends, and then to bed.

LITTLE JOHN.

What will you have, my lord?

ROBIN.

                    'To sleep! to sleep!'

LITTLE JOHN.

There is a touch of sadness in it, my lord,
But ill befitting such a festal day

ROBIN.

I have a touch of sadness in myself.
Sing.

D

SONG.

To sleep ! to sleep !   The long bright day is done,
And darkness rises from the fallen sun.
To sleep ! to sleep !
Whate'er thy joys, they vanish with the day ;
Whate'er thy griefs, in sleep they fade away.
To sleep ! to sleep !
Sleep, mournful heart, and let the past be past !
Sleep, happy soul ! all life will sleep at last.
To sleep ! to sleep !

> [*A trumpet blown at the gates.*

ROBIN.

Who breaks the stillness of the morning thus ?

LITTLE JOHN (*going out and returning*).

It is a royal messenger, my lord :
I trust he brings us news of the King's coming.

Enter a PURSUIVANT *who reads.*

O yes, O yes, O yes !   In the name of the Regent.
Thou, Robin Hood Earl of Huntingdon, art attainted
and hast lost thine earldom of Huntingdon.   More-
over thou art dispossessed of all thy lands, goods,
and chattels ; and by virtue of this writ, whereas

Robin Hood Earl of Huntingdon by force and arms hath trespassed against the king in divers manners, therefore by the judgment of the officers of the said lord king, according to the law and custom of the kingdom of England Robin Hood Earl of Huntingdon is outlawed and banished.

ROBIN.

I have shelter'd some that broke the forest laws.
This is irregular and the work of John.

> [' Irregular, irregular ! (*tumult*) Down with
> him, tear his coat from his back ! '

MESSENGER.

Ho there ! ho there, the Sheriff's men without !

ROBIN.

Nay, let them be, man, let them be.   We yield.
How should we cope with John ?   The London
    folkmote
Has made him all but king, and he hath seized
On half the royal castles.   Let him alone ! (*to his men*)
A worthy messenger ! how should he help it ?
Shall *we* too work injustice ? what, thou shakest !
Here, here—a cup of wine—drink and begone !

> [*Exit* MESSENGER.

We will away in four-and-twenty hours,
But shall we leave our England ?

TUCK.

Robin, Earl—

ROBIN.

Let be the Earl.   Henceforth I am no more
Than plain man to plain man.

TUCK.

Well, then, plain man,
There be good fellows there in merry Sherwood
That hold by Richard, tho' they kill his deer.

ROBIN.

In Sherwood Forest.   I have heard of them.
Have they no leader ?

TUCK.

Each man for his own.
Be thou their leader and they will all of them
Swarm to thy voice like bees to the brass pan.

ROBIN.

They hold by Richard—the wild wood ! to cast
All threadbare household habit, mix with all

The lusty life of wood and underwood,
Hawk, buzzard, jay, the mavis and the merle,
The tawny squirrel vaulting thro' the boughs,
The deer, the highback'd polecat, the wild boar,
The burrowing badger—By St. Nicholas
I have a sudden passion for the wild wood—
We should be free as air in the wild wood—
What say you? shall we go? Your hands, your hands!
                              [*Gives his hand to each.*
You, Scarlet, you are always moody here.

SCARLET.

'Tis for no lack of love to you, my lord,
But lack of happiness in a blatant wife.
She broke my head on Tuesday with a dish.
I would have thwack'd the woman, but I did not,
Because thou sayest such fine things of women
But I shall have to thwack her if I stay.

ROBIN.

Would it be better for thee in the wood?

SCARLET.

Ay, so she did not follow me to the wood.

ROBIN.

Then, Scarlet, thou at least wilt go with me.
Thou, Much, the miller's son, I knew thy father:

He was a manly man, as thou art, Much,
And gray before his time as thou art, Much.

MUCH.

It is the trick of the family, my lord.
There was a song he made to the turning wheel——

ROBIN.

'Turn! turn!' but I forget it.

MUCH.

I can sing it.

ROBIN.

Not now, good Much! And thou, dear Little John,
Who hast that worship for me which Heaven knows
I ill deserve—you love me, all of you,
But I am outlaw'd, and if caught, I die.
Your hands again.   All thanks for all your service;
But if you follow me, you may die with me.

ALL.

We will live and die with thee, we will live and die
with thee.

END OF ACT I.

ACT II

THE FLIGHT OF MARIAN

ACT II

SCENE 1.—*A broad forest glade, woodman's hut at one side with half-door.* FORESTERS *are looking to their bows and arrows, or polishing their swords.*

FORESTERS *sing (as they disperse to their work).*

There is no land like England
  Where'er the light of day be;
There are no hearts like English hearts
  Such hearts of oak as they be.
There is no land like England
  Where'er the light of day be;
There are no men like Englishmen
  So tall and bold as they be.

(Full chorus.)   *And these will strike for England*
                        And man and maid be free
                    To foil and spoil the tyrant
                        Beneath the greenwood tree.

            There is no land like England
                Where'er the light of day be ;
            There are no wives like English wives
                So fair and chaste as they be.
            There is no land like England
                Where'er the light of day be ;
            There are no maids like English maids
                So beautiful as they be.

(Full chorus.)   *And these shall wed with freemen,*
                    And all their sons be free,
                To sing the songs of England
                    Beneath the greenwood tree.

ROBIN (*alone*).

My lonely hour!
The king of day hath stept from off his throne,
Flung by the golden mantle of the cloud,
And sets, a naked fire.   The King of England
Perchance this day may sink as gloriously,

Red with his own and enemy's blood—but no !
We hear he is in prison.   It is my birthday.
I have reign'd one year in the wild wood. My mother,
For whose sake, and the blessed Queen of Heaven,
I reverence all women, bad me, dying,
Whene'er this day should come about, to carve
One lone hour from it, so to meditate
Upon my greater nearness to the birthday
Of the after-life, when all the sheeted dead
Are shaken from their stillness in the grave
By the last trumpet.

                  Am I worse or better ?
I am outlaw'd.   I am none the worse for that.
I held for Richard, and I hated John.
I am a thief, ay, and a king of thieves.
Ay ! but we rob the robber, wrong the wronger,
And what we wring from them we give the poor.
I am none the worse for that, and all the better
For this free forest-life, for while I sat
Among my thralls in my baronial hall
The groining hid the heavens ; but since I breathed,
A houseless head beneath the sun and stars,
The soul of the woods hath stricken thro' my blood,
The love of freedom, the desire of God,
The hope of larger life hereafter, more
Tenfold than under roof.   [*Horn blown.*
              True, were I taken

They would prick out my sight. A price is set
On this poor head ; but I believe there lives
No man who truly loves and truly rules
His following, but can keep his followers true.
I am one with mine. Traitors are rarely bred
Save under traitor kings. Our vice-king John,
True king of vice—true play on words—our John
By his Norman arrogance and dissoluteness,
Hath made *me* king of all the discontent
Of England up thro' all the forest land
North to the Tyne : being outlaw'd in a land
Where law lies dead, we make ourselves the law.
Why break you thus upon my lonely hour?

Enter LITTLE JOHN *and* KATE.

LITTLE JOHN.

I found this white doe wandering thro' the wood,
Not thine, but mine. I have shot her thro' the heart.

KATE.

He lies, my lord. I have shot *him* thro' the heart.

ROBIN.

My God, thou art the very woman who waits
On my dear Marian. Tell me, tell me of her.
Thou comest a very angel out of heaven.
Where is she? and how fares she?

KATE.

                        O my good lord,
I am but an angel by reflected light.
Your heaven is vacant of your angel.   John—
Shame on him !—
Stole on her, she was walking in the garden,
And after some slight speech about the Sheriff
He caught her round the waist, whereon she struck him,
And fled into the castle.   She and Sir Richard
Have past away, I know not where ; and I
Was left alone, and knowing as I did
That I had shot him thro' the heart, I came
To eat him up and make an end of him.

LITTLE JOHN.

In kisses ?

KATE.

        You, how dare you mention kisses ?
But I am weary pacing thro' the wood.
Show me some cave or cabin where I may rest.

ROBIN.

Go with him.   I will talk with thee anon.
              [*Exeunt* LITTLE JOHN *and* KATE.
She struck him, my brave Marian, struck the Prince,
The serpent that had crept into the garden

And coil'd himself about her sacred waist.
I think I should have stricken him to the death.
He never will forgive her.

                    O the Sheriff
Would pay this cursed mortgage to his brother
If Marian would marry him ; and the son
Is most like dead—if so the land may come
To Marian, and they rate the land five-fold
The worth of the mortgage, and who marries her
Marries the land.   Most honourable Sheriff !
(*Passionately*) Gone, and it may be gone for evermore !
O would that I could see her for a moment
Glide like a light across these woodland ways !
Tho' in one moment she should glance away,
I should be happier for it all the year.
O would she moved beside me like my shadow !
O would she stood before me as my queen,
To make this Sherwood Eden o'er again,
And these rough oaks the palms of Paradise !

    Ah ! but who be those three yonder with bows ?—
not of my band—the Sheriff, and by heaven, Prince
John himself and one of those mercenaries that suck
the blood of England.   My people are all scattered I
know not where.   Have they come for me ?   Here
is the witch's hut.   The fool-people call her a witch
—a good witch to me !   I will shelter here.

                    [*Knocks at the door of the hut.*

OLD WOMAN *comes out.*

OLD WOMAN (*kisses his hand*).

Ah dear Robin! ah noble captain, friend of the poor!

ROBIN.

I am chased by my foes. I have forgotten my horn that calls my men together. Disguise me——thy gown and thy coif.

OLD WOMAN.

Come in, come in; I would give my life for thee, for when the Sheriff had taken all our goods for the King without paying, our horse and our little cart——

ROBIN.

Quick, good mother, quick!

OLD WOMAN.

Ay, ay, gown, coif, and petticoat, and the old woman's blessing with them to the last fringe.

[*They go in.*

Enter PRINCE JOHN, SHERIFF OF NOTTINGHAM, *and* MERCENARY.

PRINCE JOHN.

Did we not hear the two would pass this way?
They must have past. Here is a woodman's hut.

MERCENARY.

Take heed, take heed! in Nottingham they say
There bides a foul witch somewhere hereabout.

SHERIFF.

Not in this hut I take it.

PRINCE JOHN.

Why not here?

SHERIFF.

I saw a man go in, my lord.

PRINCE JOHN.

Not two?

SHERIFF.

No, my lord, one.

PRINCE JOHN.

Make for the cottage then!

Interior of the hut.

ROBIN *disguised as old woman.*

PRINCE JOHN (*without*).

Knock again! knock again!

ROBIN (*to* OLD WOMAN).

Get thee into the closet there, and make a ghostly wail ever and anon to scare 'em.

OLD WOMAN.

I will, I will, good Robin.   [*Goes into closet.*

PRINCE JOHN (*without*).

Open, open, or I will drive the door from the doorpost.

ROBIN (*opens door*).

Come in, come in.

PRINCE JOHN.

Why did ye keep us at the door so long?

ROBIN (*curtseying*).

I was afear'd it was the ghost, your worship.

PRINCE JOHN.

Ghost! did one in white pass?

ROBIN (*curtseying*).

No, your worship.

PRINCE JOHN.

Did two knights pass?

E

ROBIN (*curtseying*).

No, your worship.

SHERIFF.

I fear me we have lost our labour, then.

PRINCE JOHN.

Except this old hag have been bribed to lie.

ROBIN.

We old hags should be bribed to speak truth, for, God help us, we lie by nature.

PRINCE JOHN.

There was a man just now that enter'd here?

ROBIN.

There is but one old woman in the hut.

[OLD WOMAN *yells*.

ROBIN.

I crave your worship's pardon. There is yet another old woman. She was murdered here a hundred year ago, and whenever a murder is to be done again she yells out i' this way—so they say, your worship.

MERCENARY.

Now, if I hadn't a sprig o' wickentree sewn into
my dress, I should run.

PRINCE JOHN.

Tut ! tut ! the scream of some wild woodland thing.
How came we to be parted from our men ?
We shouted, and *they* shouted, as I thought,
But shout and echo play'd into each other
So hollowly we knew not which was which.

ROBIN.

The wood is full of echoes, owls, elfs, ouphes, oafs,
ghosts o' the mist, wills-o'-the-wisp ; only they that
be bred in it can find their way a-nights in it.

PRINCE JOHN.

I am footsore and famish'd therewithal.
Is there aught there ?   [*Pointing to cupboard.*

ROBIN.

Naught for the likes o' you.

PRINCE JOHN.

Speak straight out, crookback.

ROBIN.

Sour milk and black bread.

PRINCE JOHN.

Well, set them forth.   I could eat anything.

[*He sets out a table with black bread.*

This is mere marble.   Old hag, how should thy
one tooth drill thro' this?

ROBIN.

Nay, by St. Gemini, I ha' two; and since the
Sheriff left me naught but an empty belly, they can
meet upon anything thro' a millstone.   You gentles
that live upo' manchet-bread and marchpane, what
should you know o' the food o' the poor?   Look you
here, before you can eat it you must hack it with a
hatchet, break it all to pieces, as you break the poor,
as you would hack at Robin Hood if you could light
upon him (*hacks it and flings two pieces*).   There's for
you, and there's for you—and the old woman's
welcome.

PRINCE JOHN.

The old wretch is mad, and her bread is beyond
me: and the milk—faugh!   Hast thou anything to
sweeten this?

ROBIN.

Here's a pot o' wild honey from an old oak, saving your sweet reverences.

SHERIFF.

Thou hast a cow then, hast thou?

ROBIN.

Ay, for when the Sheriff took my little horse for the King without paying for it——

SHERIFF.

How hadst thou then the means to buy a cow?

ROBIN.

Eh, I would ha' given my whole body to the King had *he* asked for it, like the woman at Acre when the Turk shot her as she was helping to build the mound against the city. I ha' served the King living, says she, and let me serve him dead, says she; let me go to make the mound: bury me in the mound, says the woman.

SHERIFF.

Ay, but the cow?

ROBIN.

She was given me.

SHERIFF.

By whom?

ROBIN.

By a thief.

SHERIFF.

Who, woman, who?

ROBIN (*sings*).

He was a forester good ;
He was the cock o' the walk ;
He was the king o' the wood.

Your worship may find another rhyme if you care
to drag your brains for such a minnow.

SHERIFF.

That cow was mine.   I have lost a cow from my
meadow.   Robin Hood was it?   I thought as much.
He will come to the gibbet at last.

[OLD WOMAN *yells.*

MERCENARY.

O sweet sir, talk not of cows.   You anger the
spirit.

PRINCE JOHN.

Anger the scritch-owl.

MERCENARY.

But, my lord, the scritch-owl bodes death, my lord.

ROBIN.

I beseech you all to speak lower.   Robin may be
hard by wi' three-score of his men.   He often looks
in here by the moonshine.   Beware of Robin.

[OLD WOMAN *yells*.

MERCENARY.

Ay, do you hear?   There may be murder done.

SHERIFF.

Have you not finished, my lord?

ROBIN.

Thou hast crost him in love, and I have heard
him swear he will be even wi' thee.

[OLD WOMAN *yells*.

MERCENARY.

Now is my heart so down in my heels that if I
stay, I can't run.

SHERIFF.

Shall we not go?

ROBIN.

And, old hag tho' I be, I can spell the hand.
Give me thine.   Ay, ay, the line o' life is marked
enow; but look, there is a cross line o' sudden death.

I pray thee go, go, for tho' thou wouldst bar me fro' the milk o' my cow, I wouldn't have thy blood on my hearth.

PRINCE JOHN.

Why do you listen, man, to the old fool?

SHERIFF.

I will give thee a silver penny if thou wilt show us the way back to Nottingham.

ROBIN (*with a very low curtsey*).

All the sweet saints bless your worship for your alms to the old woman! but make haste then, and be silent in the wood.   Follow me.

[*Takes his bow.*

(*They come out of the hut and close the door carefully.*)

Outside hut.

ROBIN.

Softly! softly! there may be a thief in every bush.

PRINCE JOHN.

How should this old lamester guide us?   Where is thy goodman?

ROBIN.

The saints were so kind to both on us that he
was dead before he was born.

PRINCE JOHN.

Half-witted and a witch to boot! Mislead us,
and 1 will have thy life! and what doest thou with
that who art more bow-bent than the very bow thou
carriest?

ROBIN.

I keep it to kill nightingales.

PRINCE JOHN.

Nightingales!

ROBIN.

You see, they are so fond o' their own voices that
I cannot sleep o' nights by cause on 'em.

PRINCE JOHN.

True soul of the Saxon churl for whom song has
no charm.

ROBIN.

Then I roast 'em, for I have nought else to live on
(*whines*). O your honour, I pray you too to give me
an alms. (*To* PRINCE JOHN.)

SHERIFF.

This is no bow to hit nightingales; this is a true
woodman's bow of the best yew-wood to slay the
deer.   Look, my lord, there goes one in the moon-
light.   Shoot!

PRINCE JOHN (*shoots*).

Missed!   There goes another.   Shoot, Sheriff!

SHERIFF (*shoots*).

Missed!

ROBIN.

And here comes another.   Why, an old woman
can shoot closer than you two.

PRINCE JOHN.

Shoot then, and if thou miss I will fasten thee to
thine own doorpost and make thine old carcase a
target for us three.

ROBIN (*raises himself upright, shoots, and hits*).

Hit!   Did I not tell you an old woman could
shoot better?

PRINCE JOHN.

Thou standest straight.   Thou speakest manlike.
Thou art no old woman—thou art disguised—thou
art one of the thieves.

[*Makes a clutch at the gown, which comes in pieces
and falls, showing* ROBIN *in his forester's dress.*

SHERIFF.

It is the very captain of the thieves!

PRINCE JOHN.

We have him at last; we have him at advantage.
Strike, Sheriff!   Strike, mercenary!

> [*They draw swords and attack him;*
> *he defends himself with his.*

Enter LITTLE JOHN.

LITTLE JOHN.

I have lodged my pretty Katekin in her bower.

How now?   Clashing of swords—three upon one,
and that one our Robin!   Rogues, have you no man-
hood?   [*Draws and defends* ROBIN.

Enter SIR RICHARD LEA (*draws his sword*).

SIR RICHARD LEA.

Old as I am, I will not brook to see
Three upon two.

> [MAID MARIAN *in the armour of a Redcross Knight*
> *follows, half unsheathing her sword and half-seen.*

Back! back! I charge thee, back!
Is this a game for thee to play at?   Away.

> [*She retires to the fringe of the copse.   He fights*
> *on* ROBIN'S *side.   The other three are beaten*
> *off and exeunt.*

Enter FRIAR TUCK.

FRIAR TUCK.

I am too late then with my quarterstaff !

ROBIN.

Quick, friar, follow them :
See whether there be more of 'em in the wood.

FRIAR TUCK.

On the gallop, on the gallop, Robin, like a deer
from a dog, or a colt from a gad-fly, or a stump-
tailed ox in May-time, or the cow that jumped over
the moon. 　　　　　　　　　　　　　　*[Exit.*

ROBIN.

Nay, nay, but softly, lest they spy thee, friar !
　　　　　[To SIR RICHARD LEA *who reels.*
Take thou mine arm.　Who art thou, gallant knight ?

SIR RICHARD.

Robin, I am Sir Richard of the Lea.
Who be those three that I have fought withal ?

ROBIN.

Prince John, the Sheriff, and a mercenary.

SIR RICHARD.

Prince John again.   We are flying from this John.
The Sheriff—I am grieved it was the Sheriff ;
For, Robin, he must be my son-in-law.
Thou art an outlaw, and couldst never pay
The mortgage on my land.   Thou wilt not see
My Marian more.   So—so—I have presumed
Beyond my strength.   Give me a draught of wine.
                              [MARIAN *comes forward.*
This is my son but late escaped from prison,
For whom I ran into my debt to the Abbot,
Two thousand marks in gold.   I have paid him half.
That other thousand—shall I ever pay it ?
A draught of wine.

ROBIN.

                    Our cellar is hard by.
Take him, good Little John, and give him wine.
        [*Exit* SIR RICHARD *leaning on* LITTLE JOHN.
A brave old fellow but he angers me.
        [*To* MAID MARIAN *who is following her father.*
Young Walter, nay, I pray thee, stay a moment.

MARIAN.

A moment for some matter of no moment !
Well—take and use your moment, while you may.

ROBIN.

Thou art her brother, and her voice is thine,

Her face is thine, and if thou be as gentle
Give me some news of my sweet Marian.
Where is she?

MARIAN.

Thy sweet Marian?   I believe
She came with me into the forest here.

ROBIN.

She follow'd thee into the forest here?

MARIAN.

Nay—that, my friend, I am sure I did not say.

ROBIN.

Thou blowest hot and cold.   Where is she then?

MARIAN.

Is she not here with thee?

ROBIN.

Would God she were!

MARIAN.

If not with thee I know not where she is.
She may have lighted on your fairies here,
And now be skipping in their fairy-rings,
And capering hand in hand with Oberon.

ROBIN.

Peace !

MARIAN.

Or learning witchcraft of your woodland witch
And how to charm and waste the hearts of men.

ROBIN.

That is not brother-like.

MARIAN (*pointing to the sky*).

Or there perchance
Up yonder with the man i' the moon.

ROBIN.

No more !

MARIAN.

Or haply fallen a victim to the wolf.

ROBIN.

Tut ! be there wolves in Sherwood ?

MARIAN.

The wolf, John !

ROBIN.

Curse him ! but thou art mocking me.   Thou art
Her brother—I forgive thee.   Come be thou
My brother too.   She loves me.

MARIAN.

Doth she so?

ROBIN.

Do you doubt me when I say she loves me, man?

MARIAN.

No, but my father will not lose his land,
Rather than that would wed her with the Sheriff.

ROBIN.

Thou hold'st with him?

MARIAN.

Yes, in some sort I do.
He is old and almost mad to keep the land.

ROBIN.

Thou hold'st with him?

MARIAN.

I tell thee, in some sort.

ROBIN (*angrily*).

Sort! sort! what sort? what sort of man art thou
For land, not love? Thou wilt inherit the land,
And so wouldst sell thy sister to the Sheriff,

O thou unworthy brother of my dear Marian !
And now, I do bethink me, thou wast by
And never drewest sword to help the old man
When he was fighting.

MARIAN.

There were three to three.

ROBIN.

Thou shouldst have ta'en his place, and fought for him.

MARIAN.

He did it so well there was no call for me.

ROBIN.

My God !
That such a brother—*she* marry the Sheriff !
Come now, I fain would have a bout with thee.
It is but pastime—nay, I will not harm thee.
Draw !

MARIAN.

Earl, I would fight with any man but thee.

ROBIN.

Ay, ay, because I have a name for prowess.

MARIAN.

It is not that.

F

ROBIN.

That ! I believe thou fell'st into the hands
Of these same Moors thro' nature's baseness, criedst
' I yield ' almost before the thing was ask'd,
And thro' thy lack of manhood hast betray'd
Thy father to the losing of his land.
Come, boy ! 'tis but to see if thou canst fence.
Draw !   [*Draws.*

MARIAN.

No, Sir Earl, I will not fight to-day.

ROBIN.

To-morrow then ?

MARIAN.

Well, I will fight to-morrow.

ROBIN.

Give me thy glove upon it.

MARIAN (*pulls off her glove and gives it to him*).

There !

ROBIN.

O God !
What sparkles in the moonlight on thy hand ?
                                    [*Takes her hand.*

In that great heat to wed her to the Sheriff
Thou hast robb'd my girl of her betrothal ring.

MARIAN.

No, no !

ROBIN.

What ! do I not know mine own ring ?

MARIAN.

I keep it for her.

ROBIN.

Nay, she swore it never
Should leave her finger.   Give it me, by heaven,
Or I will force it from thee.

MARIAN.

O Robin, Robin !

ROBIN.

O my dear Marian,
Is it thou ? is it thou ? I fall before thee, clasp
Thy knees.   I am ashamed.   Thou shalt not marry
The Sheriff, but abide with me who love thee.
     [*She moves from him, the moonlight falls upon her.*
O look ! before the shadow of these dark oaks
Thou seem'st a saintly splendour out from heaven,

Clothed with the mystic silver of her moon.
Speak but one word not only of forgiveness,
But to show thou art mortal.

MARIAN

Mortal enough,
If love for thee be mortal. Lovers hold
True love immortal. Robin, tho' I love thee,
We cannot come together in this world.
Not mortal! after death, if after death——

ROBIN.

Life, life. I know not death. Why do you vex me
With raven-croaks of death and after death?

MARIAN.

And I and he are passing overseas :
He has a friend there will advance the monies,
So now the forest lawns are all as bright
As ways to heaven, I pray thee give us guides
To lead us thro' the windings of the wood.

ROBIN.

Must it be so? If it were so, myself
Would guide you thro' the forest to the sea.
But go not yet, stay with us, and when thy brother——

MARIAN.

Robin, I ever held that saying false
That Love is blind, but thou hast proven it true.
Why—even your woodland squirrel sees the nut
Behind the shell, and thee however mask'd
I should have known.   But thou—to dream that he
My brother, my dear Walter—now, perhaps,
Fetter'd and lash'd, a galley-slave, or closed
For ever in a Moorish tower, or wreckt
And dead beneath the midland ocean, he
As gentle as he's brave—that such as he
Would wrest from me the precious ring I promised
Never to part with—No, not he, nor any.
I would have battled for it to the death.

> [*In her excitement she draws her sword.*

See, thou hast wrong'd my brother and myself.

ROBIN (*kneeling*).

See then, I kneel once more to be forgiven.

Enter SCARLET, MUCH, *several of the* FORESTERS,
rushing on.

SCARLET.

Look ! look ! he kneels ! he has anger'd the foul witch,
Who melts a waxen image by the fire,
And drains the heart and marrow from a man.

MUCH.

Our Robin beaten, pleading for his life !
Seize on the knight ! wrench his sword from him !.

> [*They all rush on* MARIAN.

ROBIN (*springing up and waving his hand*).

Back !

Back all of you ! this is Maid Marian
Flying from John—disguised.

MEN.

Maid Marian ? she ?

SCARLET.

Captain, we saw thee cowering to a knight
And thought thou wert bewitch'd.

MARIAN.

You dared to dream
That our great Earl, the bravest English heart
Since Hereward the Wake, would cower to any
Of mortal build.   Weak natures that impute
Themselves to their unlikes, and their own want
Of manhood to their leader ! he would break,
Far as he might, the power of John—but you—
What rightful cause could grow to such a heat
As burns a wrong to ashes, if the followers

Of him, who heads the movement, held him craven?
Robin—I know not, can I trust myself
With your brave band? in some of these may lodge
That baseness which for fear or monies, might
Betray me to the wild Prince.

ROBIN.

No, love, no!
Not any of these, I swear.

MEN.

No, no, we swear.

SCENE II.—*Another Glade in the Forest.*

ROBIN *and* MARIAN *passing.   Enter* FORESTER.

FORESTER.

Knight, your good father had his draught of wine
And then he swoon'd away.   He had been hurt,
And bled beneath his armour.   Now he cries
'The land! the land!'   Come to him.

MARIAN.

O my poor father!

ROBIN.

Stay with us in this wood, till he recover.
We know all balms and simples of the field
To help a wound.   Stay with us here, sweet love,
Maid Marian, till thou wed what man thou wilt.
All here will prize thee, honour, worship thee,
Crown thee with flowers ; and he will soon be well :
All will be well.

MARIAN.

O lead me to my father !
[*As they are going out enter* LITTLE JOHN *and*
KATE *who falls on the neck of* MARIAN.

KATE.

No, no, false knight, thou canst not hide thyself
From her who loves thee.

LITTLE JOHN.

What !
By all the devils in and out of Hell !
Wilt thou embrace thy sweetheart 'fore my face ?
Quick with thy sword ! the yeoman braves the knight
There ! (*strikes her with the flat of his sword*).

MARIAN (*laying about her*).

Are the men all mad ? there then, and there !

KATE.

O hold thy hand ! this is our Marian.

LITTLE JOHN.

What ! with this skill of fence ! let go mine arm

ROBIN.

Down with thy sword !   She is my queen and thine,
The mistress of the band.

MARIAN (*sheathing her sword*).

                              A maiden now
Were ill-bested in these dark days of John,
Except she could defend her innocence.
O lead me to my father.

                    [*Exeunt* ROBIN *and* MARIAN.

LITTLE JOHN.

                    Speak to me,
I am like a boy now going to be whipt ;
I know I have done amiss, have been a fool,
Speak to me, Kate, and say you pardon me !

KATE.

I never will speak word to thee again.
What ? to mistrust the girl you say you love

Is to mistrust your own love for your girl !
How should you love if you mistrust your love ?

LITTLE JOHN.

O Kate, true love and jealousy are twins,
And love is joyful, innocent, beautiful,
And jealousy is wither'd, sour and ugly :
Yet are they twins and always go together.

KATE.

Well, well, until they cease to go together,
I am but a stone and a dead stock to thee.

LITTLE JOHN.

I thought I saw thee clasp and kiss a man
And it was but a woman.   Pardon me.

KATE.

Ay, for I much disdain thee, but if ever
Thou see me clasp and kiss a man indeed,
I will again be thine, and not till then.   [*Exit.*

LITTLE JOHN.

I have been a fool and I have lost my Kate.   [*Exit.*

Re-enter ROBIN.

ROBIN.

He dozes.   I have left her watching him.
She will not marry till her father yield.
The old man dotes.
Nay—and she will not marry till Richard come,
And that's at latter Lammas—never perhaps.
Besides, tho' Friar Tuck might make us one,
An outlaw's bride may not be wife in law.
I am weary.   [*Lying down on a bank.*
What's here? a dead bat in the fairy ring—
Yes, I remember, Scarlet hacking down
A hollow ash, a bat flew out at him
In the clear noon, and hook'd him by the hair,
And he was scared and slew it.   My men say
The fairies haunt this glade ;—if one could catch
A glimpse of them and of their fairy Queen—
Have our loud pastimes driven them all away?
I never saw them : yet I could believe
There came some evil fairy at my birth
And cursed me, as the last heir of my race :
' This boy will never wed the maid he loves,
Nor leave a child behind him ' (*yawns*).   Weary—
        weary
As tho' a spell were on me (*he dreams*).
    [*The whole stage lights up, and fairies are seen swing-
        ing on boughs and nestling in hollow trunks.*

Titania *on a hill,* Fairies *on either side of her,*
the moon above the hill.

First Fairy.

Evil fairy! do you hear?
So he said who lieth here.

Second Fairy.

We be fairies of the wood,
We be neither bad nor good.

First Fairy.

Back and side and hip and rib,
Nip, nip him for his fib.

Titania.

Nip him not, but let him snore.
We must flit for evermore.

First Fairy.

Tit, my queen, must it be so?
Wherefore, wherefore should we go?

Titania.

I Titania bid you flit,
And you dare to call me Tit.

FIRST FAIRY.

Tit, for love and brevity,
Not for love of levity.

TITANIA.

Pertest of our flickering mob,
Wouldst thou call my Oberon Ob?

FIRST FAIRY.

Nay, an please your Elfin Grace,
Never Ob before his face.

TITANIA.

Fairy realm is breaking down
When the fairy slights the crown.

FIRST FAIRY.

No, by wisp and glowworm, no.
Only wherefore should we go?

TITANIA.

We must fly from Robin Hood
And this new queen of the wood.

FIRST FAIRY.

True, she is a goodly thing.
Jealousy, jealousy of the king.

TITANIA.

Nay, for Oberon fled away
Twenty thousand leagues to-day.

CHORUS.

Look, there comes a deputation
From our finikin fairy nation.

Enter several FAIRIES.

THIRD FAIRY.

Crush'd my bat whereon I flew !
Found him dead and drench'd in dew,
Queen.

FOURTH FAIRY.

Quash'd my frog that used to quack
When I vaulted on his back,
Queen.

FIFTH FAIRY.

Kill'd the sward where'er they sat,
Queen.

SIXTH FAIRY.

Lusty bracken beaten flat,
Queen.

Seventh Fairy.

Honest daisy deadly bruised,
                    Queen.

Eighth Fairy.

Modest maiden lily abused,
                    Queen.

Ninth Fairy.

Beetle's jewel armour crack'd,
                    Queen.

Tenth Fairy.

Reed I rock'd upon broken-back'd,
                    Queen.

Fairies (*in chorus*).

We be scared with song and shout.
Arrows whistle all about.
All our games be put to rout.
All our rings be trampled out.
Lead us thou to some deep glen,
Far from solid foot of men,
Never to return again,
                    Queen.

TITANIA (*to* FIRST FAIRY).

Elf, with spiteful heart and eye,
Talk of jealousy?   You see why
We must leave the wood and fly.

(*To all the* FAIRIES, *who sing at intervals with*
TITANIA.)

Up with you, out of the forest and over the hills and
   away,
And over this Robin Hood's bay!
Up thro' the light of the seas by the moon's long-silvering
   ray!
To a land where the fay,
Not an eye to survey,
In the night, in the day,
Can have frolic and play.
Up with you, all of you, out of it! hear and obey.
Man, lying here alone,
Moody creature,
Of a nature
Stronger, sadder than my own,
Were I human, were I human,
I could love you like a woman.
Man, man,
You shall wed your Marian.
She is true, and you are true,
And you love her and she loves you;

Both be happy, and adieu for ever and for evermore—
   adieu.

ROBIN (*half waking*).

Shall I be happy ?   Happy vision, stay.

TITANIA.

Up with you, all of you, off with you, out of it, over the
   wood and away !

END OF ACT II

ACT III

THE CROWNING OF MARIAN

ACT III

SCENE I.—*Heart of the forest.*

MARIAN *and* KATE (*in Foresters' green*).

KATE.

What makes you seem so cold to Robin, lady?

MARIAN.

What makes thee think I seem so cold to Robin?

KATE.

You never whisper close as lovers do,
Nor care to leap into each other's arms.

MARIAN.

There is a fence I cannot overleap,
My father's will.

KATE.

Then you will wed the Sheriff?

MARIAN.

When heaven falls, I may light on such a lark!
But who art thou to catechize me——thou
That hast not made it up with Little John!

KATE.

I wait till Little John makes up to *me*.

MARIAN.

Why, my good Robin fancied me a man,
And drew his sword upon me, and Little John
Fancied he saw thee clasp and kiss a man.

KATE.

Well, if *he* fancied that *I* fancy a man
Other than *him*, he is *not* the man for me.

MARIAN.

And that would quite *un*man him, heart and soul.
For both are thine
          (*Looking up.*)
               But listen——overhead——

Fluting, and piping and luting ' Love, love, love '——
Those sweet tree-Cupids half-way up in heaven,
The birds—would I were one of 'em ! O good Kate—
If my man-Robin were but a bird-Robin,
How happily would we lilt among the leaves
' Love, love, love, love '—what merry madness—listen !
And let them warm thy heart to Little John.
Look where he comes !

KATE.

                    I will not meet him yet,
I'll watch him from behind the trees, but call
Kate when you will, for I am close at hand.

KATE *stands aside and enter* ROBIN, *and after him at
    a little distance* LITTLE JOHN, MUCH *the Miller's
    son, and* SCARLET *with an oaken chaplet, and
    other* FORESTERS.

LITTLE JOHN.

My lord—Robin—I crave pardon—you always
seem to me my lord—I Little John, he Much the
miller's son, and he Scarlet, honouring all womankind,
and more especially my lady Marian, do here, in the
name of all our woodmen, present her with this
oaken chaplet as Queen of the wood, I Little John,

he, young Scarlet, and he, old Much, and all the rest
of us.

MUCH.

And I, old Much, say as much, for being every
inch a man I honour every inch of a woman.

ROBIN.

Friend Scarlet, art thou less a man than Much?
Why art thou mute? Dost thou not honour woman?

SCARLET.

Robin, I do, but I have a bad wife.

ROBIN.

Then let her pass as an exception, Scarlet.

SCARLET.

So I would, Robin, if any man would accept her.

MARIAN (*puts on the chaplet*).

Had I a bulrush now in this right hand
For sceptre, I were like a queen indeed.
Comrades, I thank you for your loyalty,
And take and wear this symbol of your love;
And were my kindly father sound again,
Could live as happy as the larks in heaven,

And join your feasts and all your forest games
As far as maiden might.   Farewell, good fellows!

> [*Exeunt several* FORESTERS, *the others withdraw
>   to the back.*

ROBIN.

Sit here by me, where the most beaten track
Runs thro' the forest, hundreds of huge oaks,
Gnarl'd—older than the thrones of Europe—look,
What breadth, height, strength—torrents of eddying
       bark !
Some hollow-hearted from exceeding age—
That never be thy lot or mine !—and some
Pillaring a leaf-sky on their monstrous boles,
Sound at the core as we are.   Fifty leagues
Of woodland hear and know my horn, that scares
The Baron at the torture of his churls,
The pillage of his vassals.

                   O maiden-wife,
The oppression of our people moves me so,
That when I think of it hotly, Love himself
Seems but a ghost, but when thou feel'st with me
The ghost returns to Marian, clothes itself
In maiden flesh and blood, and looks at once
Maid Marian, and that maiden freedom which
Would never brook the tyrant.   Live thou maiden !
Thou art more my wife so feeling, than if my wife

And siding with these proud priests, and these
    Barons,
Devils, that make this blessed England hell.

MARIAN.

Earl——

ROBIN.

    Nay, no Earl am I.   I am English yeoman.

MARIAN.

Then *I* am yeo-woman.   O the clumsy word!

ROBIN.

Take thou this light kiss for thy clumsy word.
Kiss me again.

MARIAN.

       Robin, I will not kiss thee,
For that belongs to marriage; but I hold thee
The husband of my heart, the noblest light
That ever flash'd across my life, and I
Embrace thee with the kisses of the soul.

ROBIN.

I thank thee.

MARIAN.

      Scarlet told me——is it true?——
That John last week return'd to Nottingham,
And all the foolish world is pressing thither.

ROBIN.

Sit here, my queen, and judge the world with me.
Doubtless, like judges of another bench,
However wise, we must at times have wrought
Some great injustice, yet, far as we knew,
We never robb'd one friend of the true King.
We robb'd the traitors that are leagued with John;
We robb'd the lawyer who went against the law;
We spared the craftsman, chapman, all that live
By their own hands, the labourer, the poor priest;
We spoil'd the prior, friar, abbot, monk,
For playing upside down with Holy Writ.
'Sell all thou hast and give it to the poor;'
Take all they have and give it to thyself!
Then after we have eased them of their coins
It is our forest custom they should revel
Along with Robin.

MARIAN.

And if a woman pass——

ROBIN.

Dear, in these days of Norman license, when
Our English maidens are their prey, if ever
A Norman damsel fell into our hands,
In this dark wood when all was in our power
We never wrong'd a woman.

MARIAN.

Noble Robin.

LITTLE JOHN (*coming forward*).

Here come three beggars.

Enter the three BEGGARS.

LITTLE JOHN.

Toll !

FIRST BEGGAR.

Eh ! we be beggars, we come to ask o' you.   We
ha' nothing.

SECOND BEGGAR.

Rags, nothing but our rags.

THIRD BEGGAR.

I have but one penny in pouch, and so you would
make it two I should be grateful.

MARIAN.

Beggars, you are sturdy rogues that should be set
to work.   You are those that tramp the country, filch
the linen from the hawthorn, poison the house-dog,

and scare lonely maidens at the farmstead.   Search them, Little John.

LITTLE JOHN.

These two have forty gold marks between them, Robin.

ROBIN.

Cast them into our treasury, the beggars' mites. Part shall go to the almshouses at Nottingham, part to the shrine of our Lady.   Search this other.

LITTLE JOHN.

He hath, as he said, but one penny.

ROBIN.

Leave it with him and add a gold mark thereto. He hath spoken truth in a world of lies.

THIRD BEGGAR.

I thank you, my lord.

LITTLE JOHN.

A fine, a fine! he hath called plain Robin a lord. How much for a beggar?

ROBIN.

Take his penny and leave him his gold mark.

LITTLE JOHN.

Sit there, knaves, till the captain call for you.

[*They pass behind the trunk of an oak on the right.*

MARIAN.

Art thou not hard upon them, my good Robin?

ROBIN.

They might be harder upon thee, if met in a black lane at midnight : the throat might gape before the tongue could cry who?

LITTLE JOHN.

Here comes a citizen, and I think his wife.

Enter CITIZEN *and* WIFE.

CITIZEN.

That business which we have in Nottingham——

LITTLE JOHN.

Halt!

CITIZEN.

O dear wife, we have fallen into the hands
Of Robin Hood.

MARIAN.

           And Robin Hood hath sworn—
Shame on thee, Little John, thou hast forgotten—
That by the blessed Mother no man, so
His own true wife came with him, should be stay'd
From passing onward.   Fare you well, fair lady!

                    [Bowing to her.

ROBIN.

And may your business thrive in Nottingham!

CITIZEN.

I thank you, noble sir, the very blossom
Of bandits.   Curtsey to him, wife, and thank him.

WIFE.

I thank you, noble sir, and will pray for you
That *you* may thrive, but in some kindlier trade.

CITIZEN.

Away, away, wife, wilt thou anger him?

             [Exeunt CITIZEN *and his* WIFE.

LITTLE JOHN.

Here come three friars.

ROBIN.

Marian, thou and thy woman (*looking round*),
Why, where is Kate?

MARIAN (*calling*).

Kate!

KATE.

Here!

ROBIN.

Thou and thy woman are a match for three
friars. Take thou my bow and arrow and compel
them to pay toll.

MARIAN.

Toll!

Enter three FRIARS.

FIRST FRIAR (*advancing*).

Behold a pretty Dian of the wood,
Prettier than that same widow which you wot of.
Ha, brother.   Toll, my dear? the toll of love.

MARIAN (*drawing bow*).

Back! how much money hast thou in thy purse?

FIRST FRIAR.

Thou art playing with us. How should poor friars
have money?

MARIAN.

How much? how much?   Speak, or the arrow flies.

FIRST FRIAR.

How much? well, now I bethink me, I have one mark in gold which a pious son of the Church gave me this morning on my setting forth.

MARIAN (*bending bow at the second*).

And thou?

SECOND FRIAR.

Well, as he said, one mark in gold.

MARIAN (*bending bow at the third*).

And thou?

THIRD FRIAR.

One mark in gold.

· MARIAN.

Search them, Kate, and see if they have spoken truth.

KATE.

They are all mark'd men.   They have told but a tenth of the truth : they have each ten marks in gold.

H

MARIAN.

Leave them each what they say is theirs, and take
the twenty-seven marks to the captain's treasury.
Sit there till you be called for.

FIRST FRIAR.

We have fall'n into the hands of Robin Hood.

[MARIAN *and* KATE *return to* ROBIN.
[*The* FRIARS *pass behind an oak on the left.*

ROBIN.

Honour to thee, brave Marian, and thy Kate.
I know them arrant knaves in Nottingham.
One half of this shall go to those they have wrong'd,
One half shall pass into our treasury.
Where lies that cask of wine whereof we plunder'd
The Norman prelate?

LITTLE JOHN.

                In that oak, where twelve
Can stand upright, nor touch each other.

ROBIN.

                                Good!
Roll it in here.   These friars, thieves, and liars,
Shall drink the health of our new woodland Queen.

And they shall pledge thee, Marian, loud enough
To fright the wild swan passing overhead,
The mouldwarp underfoot.

MARIAN.

                    They pledge me, Robin?
The silent blessing of one honest man
Is heard in heaven—the wassail yells of thief
And rogue and liar echo down in Hell,
And wake the Devil, and I may sicken by 'em.
Well, well, be it so, thou strongest thief of all,
For thou hast stolen my will, and made it thine.

FRIAR TUCK, LITTLE JOHN, MUCH,
and SCARLET *roll in cask.*

FRIAR TUCK.

I marvel is it sack or Malvoisie?

ROBIN.

Do me the service to tap it, and thou wilt know.

FRIAR TUCK.

I would tap myself in thy service, Robin.

ROBIN.

And thou wouldst run more wine than blood.

FRIAR TUCK.

And both at thy service, Robin.

ROBIN.

I believe thee, thou art a good fellow, though a
friar.   [*They pour the wine into cups.*

FRIAR TUCK.

Fill to the brim.   Our Robin, King o' the woods,
Wherever the horn sound, and the buck bound,
Robin, the people's friend, the King o' the woods!
                              [*They drink.*

ROBIN.

To the brim and over till the green earth drink
Her health along with us in this rich draught,
And answer it in flowers.   The Queen o' the woods,
Wherever the buck bound, and the horn sound,
Maid Marian, Queen o' the woods!   [*They drink.*
                        Here, you three rogues,
            [*To the* BEGGARS.   *They come out.*
You caught a lonely woodman of our band,
And bruised him almost to the death, and took
His monies.

THIRD BEGGAR.

Captain, nay, it wasn't me.

ROBIN.

You ought to dangle up there among the crows.
Drink to the health of our new Queen o' the woods,
Or else be bound and beaten.

FIRST BEGGAR.

             Sir, sir—well,
We drink the health of thy new Queen o' the woods.

ROBIN.

Louder! louder! Maid Marian, Queen o' the woods!

BEGGARS (*shouting*).

Maid Marian, Queen o' the woods: Queen o' the
woods!

FIRST *and* SECOND BEGGARS (*aside*).

The black fiend grip her!

                 [*They drink.*

ROBIN (*to the* FRIARS).

          And you three holy men,
            [*They come out.*
You worshippers of the Virgin, one of you
Shamed a too trustful widow whom you heard
In her confession; and another—worse!—
An innocent maid. Drink to the Queen o' the woods,
Or else be bound and beaten.

FIRST FRIAR.

Robin Hood,
These be the lies the people tell of us,
Because we seek to curb their viciousness.
However—to this maid, this Queen o' the woods.

ROBIN.

Louder, louder, ye knaves.   Maid Marian!
Queen o' the woods!

FRIARS (*shouting*).

Maid Marian, Queen o' the woods.

FIRST FRIAR (*aside*).

Maid?

SECOND FRIAR (*aside*).

Paramour!

THIRD FRIAR (*aside*).

Hell take her!

[*They drink.*

FRIAR TUCK.

Robin, will you not hear one of these beggars'
catches? They can do it. I have heard 'em in the
market at Mansfield.

LITTLE JOHN.

No, my lord, hear ours—Robin—I crave pardon,
I always think of you as my lord, but I may still say
my lady; and, my lady, Kate and I have fallen out
again, and I pray you to come between us again, for,
my lady, we have made a song in your honour, so
your ladyship care to listen.

ROBIN.

Sing, and by St. Mary these beggars and these
friars shall join you.   Play the air, Little John.

LITTLE JOHN.

Air and word, my lady, are maid and man.   Join
them and they are a true marriage; and so, I pray
you, my lady, come between me and my Kate and
make us one again.   Scarlet, begin.

> [*Playing the air on his viol.*

SCARLET.

By all the deer that spring
Thro' wood and lawn and ling,
 When all the leaves are green;
By arrow and gray goosewing,
When horn and echo ring,
We care so much for a King;
 We care not much for a Queen—
  For a Queen, for a Queen o' the woods.

MARIAN.

Do you call that in my honour?

SCARLET.

Bitters before dinner, my lady, to give you a relish.
The first part—made before you came among us—
they put it upon me because I have a bad wife.   I
love you all the same.   Proceed.   [*All the rest sing.*

> *By all the leaves of spring,*
> *And all the birds that sing*
> *   When all the leaves are green ;*
> *By arrow and by bowstring,*
> *We care so much for a King*
> *   That we would die for a Queen—*
> *   For a Queen, for a Queen o' the woods.*

Enter FORESTER.

FORESTER.

Black news, black news from Nottingham ! I grieve
I am the Raven who croaks it.   My lord John,
In wrath because you drove him from the forest,
Is coming with a swarm of mercenaries
To break our band and scatter us to the winds.

MARIAN.

O Robin, Robin !   See that men be set

Along the glades and passes of the wood
To warn us of his coming! then each man
That owns a wife or daughter, let him bury her
Even in the bowels of the earth to 'scape
The glance of John——

ROBIN.

You hear your Queen, obey!

END OF ACT III

ACT IV

THE CONCLUSION

ACT IV

SCENE.—*A forest bower, cavern in background.*
Sunrise.

MARIAN (*rising to meet Robin*).

Robin, the sweet light of a mother's eye,
That beam of dawn upon the opening flower,
Has never glanced upon me when a child.
He was my father, mother, both in one.
The love that children owe to both I give
To him alone.

(ROBIN *offers to caress her.*)

MARIAN.

Quiet, good Robin, quiet!
You lovers are such clumsy summer-flies
For ever buzzing at your lady's face.

ROBIN.

Bees rather, flying to the flower for honey.

MARIAN (*sings*).

The bee buzz'd up in the heat.
' I am faint for your honey, my sweet.'
The flower said ' Take it, my dear,
For now is the spring of the year.
    So come, come ! '
      ' Hum ! '
And the bee buzz'd down from the heat.

And the bee buzz'd up in the cold
When the flower was wither'd and old.
' Have you still any honey, my dear ? '
She said ' It's the fall of the year,
    But come, come ! '
      ' Hum ! '
And the bee buzz'd off in the cold.

ROBIN.

Out on thy song !

MARIAN.

Did I not sing it in tune ?

ROBIN.

No, sweetheart ! out of tune with Love and me.

MARIAN.

And yet in tune with Nature and the bees.

ROBIN.

Out on it, I say, as out of tune and time!

MARIAN.

Till thou thyself shalt come to sing it—in time.

ROBIN (*taking a tress of her hair in his hand*).
Time! if his backward-working alchemy
Should change this gold to silver, why, the silver
Were dear as gold, the wrinkle as the dimple.
Thy bee should buzz about the Court of John.
No ribald John is Love, no wanton Prince,
The ruler of an hour, but lawful King,
Whose writ will run thro' all the range of life.
Out upon all hard-hearted maidenhood!

MARIAN.

And out upon all simple batchelors!
Ah, well! thou seest the land has come between us,
And my sick father here has come between us,
And this rich Sheriff too has come between us;
So, is it not all over now between us?
Gone, like a deer that hath escaped thine arrow!

ROBIN.

What deer when I have mark'd him ever yet
Escaped mine arrow? over is it? wilt thou
Give me thy hand on that?

MARIAN.

Take it.

ROBIN (*kisses her hand*).

The Sheriff!

This ring cries out against thee.   Say it again,
And by this ring the lips that never breathed
Love's falsehood to true maid will seal Love's truth
On those sweet lips that dare to dally with it.

MARIAN.

Quiet, quiet! or I will to my father.

ROBIN.

So, then, thy father will not grace our feast
With his white beard to-day.

MARIAN.

Being so sick

How should he, Robin?

ROBIN.

Then that bond he hath
Of the Abbot——wilt thou ask him for it?

MARIAN.

Why?

ROBIN.

I have sent to the Abbot and justiciary
To bring their counter-bond into the forest.

MARIAN.

But will they come?

ROBIN.

                    If not I have let them know
Their lives unsafe in any of these our woods,
And in the winter I will fire their farms.
But I have sworn by our Lady if they come
I will not tear the bond, but see fair play
Betwixt them and Sir Richard—promised too,
So that they deal with us like honest men,
They shall be handled with all courteousness.

MARIAN.

What wilt thou do with the bond then?

ROBIN.

                              Wait and see.
What wilt thou do with the Sheriff?

MARIAN.

                    Wait and see.
I bring the bond.   [*Exit* MARIAN.

I

Enter LITTLE JOHN, FRIAR TUCK, *and* MUCH, *and*
FORESTERS *and* PEASANTS *laughing and talking*.

ROBIN.

Have ye glanced down thro' all the forest ways
And mark'd if those two knaves from York be
    coming?

LITTLE JOHN.

Not yet, but here comes one of bigger mould.
                              [*Enter* KING RICHARD.
Art thou a knight?

KING RICHARD.

                    I am.

ROBIN.

                              And walkest here
Unarmour'd? all these walks are Robin Hood's
And sometimes perilous.

KING RICHARD.

                    Good! but having lived
For twenty days and nights in mail, at last
I crawl'd like a sick crab from my old shell,
That I might breathe for a moment free of shield
And cuirass in this forest where I dream'd

That all was peace—not even a Robin Hood—
(*Aside*) What if these knaves should know me for
   their King?

ROBIN.

Art thou for Richard, or allied to John?

KING RICHARD.

I *am* allied to John.

ROBIN.

   The worse for thee.

KING RICHARD.

Art thou that banish'd lord of Huntingdon,
The chief of these outlaws who break the law?

ROBIN.

I am the yeoman, plain Robin Hood, and being
out of the law how should we break the law? if we
broke into it again we should break the law, and then
we were no longer outlaws.

KING RICHARD.

But, Earl, if thou be he——

FRIAR TUCK.

Fine him! fine him! he hath called plain Robin
an earl.   How much is it, Robin, for a knight?

ROBIN.

A mark.

KING RICHARD (*gives it*).

There.

ROBIN.

Thou payest easily, like a good fellow,
But being o' John's side we must have thy gold.

KING RICHARD.

But I am more for Richard than for John.

ROBIN.

What, what, a truckler ! a word-eating coward !
Nay, search him then.   How much hast thou about
    thee ?

KING RICHARD.

I had one mark.

ROBIN.

What more ?

KING RICHARD.

                  No more, I think.
But how then if I will not bide to be search'd ?

ROBIN.

We are four to one.

King Richard.

  And I might deal with four.

Robin.

Good, good, I love thee for that! but if I wind
This forest-horn of mine I can bring down
Fourscore tall fellows on thee.

King Richard.

     Search me then.
I should be hard beset with thy fourscore.

Little John (*searching* King Richard).

Robin, he hath no more. He hath spoken truth.

Robin.

I am glad of it. Give him back his gold again.

King Richard.

But I had liefer than this gold again—
Not having broken fast the livelong day—
Something to eat.

Robin.

  And thou shalt have it, man.
Our feast is yonder, spread beneath an oak,

Venison, and wild boar, wild goose, besides
Hedge-pigs, a savoury viand, so thou be
Squeamish at eating the King's venison.

KING RICHARD.

Nay, Robin, I am like thyself in that
I look on the King's venison as my own.

FRIAR TUCK.

Ay, ay, Robin, but let him know our forest laws:
he that pays not for his dinner must fight for it.   In
the sweat of thy brow, says Holy Writ, shalt thou
eat bread, but in the sweat of thy brow and thy breast,
and thine arms, and thy legs, and thy heart, and thy
liver, and in the fear of thy life shalt thou eat the
King's venison—ay, and so thou fight at quarterstaff
for thy dinner with our Robin, that will give thee a
new zest for it, though thou wert like a bottle full up
to the cork, or as hollow as a kex, or the shambles-
oak, or a weasel-sucked egg, or the head of a fool, or
the heart of Prince John, or any other symbol of
vacuity.

[*They bring out the quarterstaffs, and the* FORESTERS
and PEASANTS *crowd round to see the games, and
applaud at intervals.*

KING RICHARD.

Great woodland king, I know not quarterstaff.

LITTLE JOHN.

A fine! a fine! He hath called plain Robin a king.

ROBIN.

A shadow, a poetical fiction—did ye not call me king in your song?—a mere figure. Let it go by.

FRIAR TUCK.

No figure, no fiction, Robin. What, is not man a hunting animal? And look you now, if we kill a stag, our dogs have their paws cut off, and the hunters, if caught, are blinded, or worse than blinded. Is that to be a king? If the king and the law work injustice, is not he that goes against the king and the law the true king in the sight of the King of kings? Thou art the king of the forest, and I would thou wert the king of the land.

KING RICHARD.

This friar is of much boldness, noble captain.

ROBIN.

He hath got it from the bottle, noble knight.

FRIAR TUCK.

Boldness out of the bottle! I defy thee.
Boldness is in the blood, Truth in the bottle.

She lay so long at the bottom of her well
In the cold water that she lost her voice,
And so she glided up into the heart
O' the bottle, the warm wine, and found it again.
In vino veritas.   Shall I undertake
The knight at quarterstaff, or thou?

ROBIN.

Peace, magpie!
Give him the quarterstaff.   Nay, but thyself
Shalt play a bout with me, that he may see
The fashion of it.

   [*Plays with* LITTLE JOHN *at quarterstaff.*

KING RICHARD.

   Well, then, let me try.   [*They play.*
I yield, I yield.   I know no quarterstaff.

ROBIN.

Then thou shalt play the game of buffets with us.

KING RICHARD.

What's that?

ROBIN.

I stand up here, thou there.   I give thee
A buffet, and thou me.   The Holy Virgin

Stand by the strongest.   I am overbreathed,
Friar, by my two bouts at quarterstaff.
Take him and try him, friar.

Friar Tuck.

There !   [*Strikes.*

King Richard (*strikes*).

There !   [Friar *falls.*

Friar Tuck.

There !

Thou hast roll'd over the Church militant
Like a tod of wool from wagon into warehouse.
Nay, I defy thee still.   Try me an hour hence.
I am misty with my thimbleful of ale.

Robin.

Thou seest, Sir Knight, our friar is so holy
That he's a miracle-monger, and can make
Five quarts pass into a thimble.   Up, good Much.

Friar Tuck.

And show thyself more of a man than me.

Much.

Well, no man yet has ever bowl'd me down.

SCARLET.

Ay, for old Much is every inch a man.

ROBIN.

We should be all the more beholden to him.

MUCH.

Much and more! much and more! I am the oldest of thy men, and thou and thy youngsters are always muching and moreing me.

ROBIN.

Because thou art always so much more of a man than my youngsters, old Much.

MUCH.

Well, we Muches be old.

ROBIN.

Old as the hills.

MUCH.

Old as the mill. We had it i' the Red King's time, and so I *may* be more of a man than to be bowled over like a ninepin. There! [*Strikes.*

KING RICHARD.

There! [MUCH *falls.*

ROBIN.

'Much would have more,' says the proverb; but
Much hath had more than enough.   Give me thy
hand, Much; I love thee (*lifts him up*).   At him,
Scarlet!

SCARLET.

I cannot cope with him : my wrist is strain'd.

KING RICHARD.

Try, thyself, valorous Robin !

ROBIN.

I am mortally afear'd o' thee, thou big man,
But seeing valour is one against all odds,
There !

KING RICHARD.

There !   [ROBIN *falls back, and is caught in
                    the arms of* LITTLE JOHN.

ROBIN.

Good, now I love thee mightily, thou tall fellow.
Break thine alliance with this faithless John,
And live with us and the birds in the green wood.

KING RICHARD.

I cannot break it, Robin, if I wish'd.
Still I am more for Richard than for John.

LITTLE JOHN.

Look, Robin, at the far end of the glade
I see two figures crawling up the hill.
                    [*Distant sound of trumpets.*

ROBIN.

The Abbot of York and his justiciary.

KING RICHARD (*aside*).

They know me.   I must not as yet be known.
Friends, your free sports have swallow'd my free
      hour.
Farewell at once, for I must hence upon
The King's affair.
                    ROBIN.

                    Not taste his venison first?

FRIAR TUCK.

Hast thou not fought for it, and earn'd it?   Stay,
Dine with my brethren here, and on thine own.

KING RICHARD.

And which be they?

FRIAR TUCK.

Wild geese, for how canst thou be thus allied
With John, and serve King Richard save thou be

A traitor or a goose ? but stay with Robin ;
For Robin is no scatterbrains like Richard,
Robin's a wise man, Richard a wiseacre,
Robin's an outlaw, but he helps the poor.
While Richard hath outlaw'd himself, and helps
Nor rich, nor poor.   Richard's the king of courtesy,
For if he did me the good grace to kick me
I could but sneak and smile and call it courtesy,
For he's a king.
And that is only courtesy _by_ courtesy—
But Robin is a thief of courtesy
Whom they that suffer by·him call the blossom
Of bandits.   There—to be a thief of courtesy—
There is a trade of genius, there's glory !
Again, this Richard sacks and wastes a town
With random pillage, but our Robin takes
From whom he knows are hypocrites and liars.
Again this Richard risks his life for a straw,
So lies in prison—while our Robin's life
Hangs by a thread, but he is a free man.
Richard, again, is king over a realm
He hardly knows, and Robin king of Sherwood,
And loves and doats on every dingle of it.
Again this Richard is the lion of Cyprus,
Robin, the lion of Sherwood—may this mouth
Never suck grape again, if our true Robin
Be not the nobler lion of the twain.

KING RICHARD.

Gramercy for thy preachment! if the land
Were ruleable by tongue, thou shouldst be king.
And yet thou know'st how little of thy king!
What was this realm of England, all the crowns
Of all this world, to Richard when he flung
His life, heart, soul into those holy wars
That sought to free the tomb-place of the King
Of all the world? thou, that art churchman too
In a fashion, and shouldst feel with him.   Farewell!
I left mine horse and armour with a Squire,
And I must see to 'em.

ROBIN.

                    When wilt thou return?

KING RICHARD.

Return, I? when? when Richard will return.

ROBIN.

No sooner? when will that be? canst thou tell?
But I have ta'en a sudden fancy to thee.
Accept this horn! if e'er thou be assail'd
In any of our forests, blow upon it
Three mots, this fashion—listen! (*blows*) Canst thou
        do it?   [KING RICHARD *blows.*
Blown like a true son of the woods.   Farewell!
                    [*Exit* KING RICHARD.

Enter ABBOT *and* JUSTICIARY.

FRIAR TUCK.

Church and Law, halt and pay toll!

JUSTICIARY.

Rogue, we have thy captain's safe-conduct; though he be the chief of rogues, he hath never broken his word.

ABBOT.

There is our bond.

               [Gives it to ROBIN.

ROBIN.

I thank thee.

JUSTICIARY.

               Ay, but where,
Where is this old Sir Richard of the Lea?
Thou told'st us we should meet him in the forest,
Where he would pay us down his thousand marks.

ROBIN.

Give him another month, and he will pay it.

JUSTICIARY.

We cannot give a month.

ROBIN.

Why then a week.

JUSTICIARY.

No, not an hour: the debt is due to-day.

ABBOT.

Where is this laggard Richard of the Lea?

ROBIN.

He hath been hurt, was growing whole again,
Only this morning in his agony
Lest he should fail to pay these thousand marks
He is stricken with a slight paralysis.
Have you no pity? must you see the man?

JUSTICIARY.

Ay, ay, what else? how else can this be settled?

ROBIN.

Go men, and fetch him hither on the litter.
                    [SIR RICHARD LEA *is brought in.*
                        MARIAN *comes with him.*

MARIAN.

Here is my father's bond.   [*Gives it to* ROBIN HOOD.

ROBIN.

I thank thee, dear.

JUSTICIARY.

Sir Richard, it was agreed when you borrowed
these monies from the Abbot that if they were not
repaid within a limited time your land should be
forfeit.

SIR RICHARD.

The land ! the land.

MARIAN.

You see he is past himself.
What would you more ?

ABBOT.

What more ? one thousand marks,
Or else the land.
You hide this damsel in your forest here,

[Pointing to MARIAN.

You hope to hold and keep her for yourself,
You heed not how you soil her maiden fame,
You scheme against her father's weal and hers,
For so this maid would wed our brother, he
Would pay us all the debt at once, and thus
This old Sir Richard might redeem his land.
He is all for love, he cares not for the land.

K

Sir Richard.

The land, the land !

Robin (*giving two bags to the* Abbot).

Here be one thousand marks
Out of our treasury to redeem the land.
                    [*Pointing to each of the bags.*
Half here, half there.   [*Plaudits from his band.*

Justiciary.

Ay, ay, but there is use, four hundred marks.

Robin (*giving a bag to* Justiciary).

There then, four hundred marks.   [*Plaudits.*

Justiciary.

What did I say ?
Nay, my tongue tript—five hundred marks for use.

Robin (*giving another bag to him*).

A hundred more ?   There then, a hundred more.
                              [*Plaudits.*

Justiciary.

Ay, ay, but you see the bond and the letter of the
law.   It is stated there that these monies should be
paid in to the Abbot at York, at the end of the
month at noon, and they are delivered here in the
wild wood an hour after noon.

MARIAN.

The letter—O how often justice drowns
Between the law and letter of the law !
O God, I would the letter of the law
Were some strong fellow here in the wild wood,
That thou mightst beat him down at quarterstaff !
Have you no pity ?

JUSTICIARY.

                    You run down your game,
We ours.   What pity have you for your game ?

ROBIN.

We needs must live.   Our bowmen are so true
They strike the deer at once to death—he falls
And knows no more.

MARIAN.

Pity, pity !—There was a man of ours
Up in the north, a goodly fellow too,
He met a stag there on so narrow a ledge—
A precipice above, and one below—
There was no room to advance or to retire.
The man lay down—the delicate-footed creature
Came stepping o'er him, so as not to harm him—
The hunter's passion flash'd into the man,
He drove his knife into the heart of the deer,
The deer fell dead to the bottom, and the man

Fell with him, and was crippled ever after.
I fear I had small pity for that man.——
You have the monies and the use of them.
What would you more ?

JUSTICIARY.

What ? must we dance attendance all the day ?

ROBIN.

Dance ! ay, by all the saints and all the devils ye shall dance. When the Church and the law have forgotten God's music, they shall dance to the music of the wild wood. Let the birds sing, and do you dance to their song. What, you will not ? Strike up our music, Little John. (*He plays.*) They will not ! Prick 'em in the calves with the arrow-points— prick 'em in the calves.

ABBOT.

Rogue, I am full of gout. I cannot dance.

ROBIN.

And Sir Richard cannot redeem his land. Sweat out your gout, friend, for by my life, you shall dance till he can. Prick him in the calves !

JUSTICIARY.

Rogue, I have a swollen vein in my right leg, and if thou prick me there I shall die.

ROBIN.

Prick him where thou wilt, so that he dance.

ABBOT.

Rogue, we come not alone.

JUSTICIARY.

Not the right.

ABBOT.

We told the Prince and the Sheriff of our coming.

JUSTICIARY.

Take the left leg for the love of God.

ABBOT.

They follow us.

JUSTICIARY.

You will all of you hang.

ROBIN.

Let us hang, so thou dance meanwhile; or by that same love of God we will hang *thee*, prince or no prince, sheriff or no sheriff.

JUSTICIARY.

Take care, take care ! I dance—I will dance—I
dance. [ABBOT *and* JUSTICIARY *dance to music,*
each holding a bag in each hand.

Enter SCARLET.

SCARLET.

The Sheriff ! the Sheriff, follow'd by Prince John
And all his mercenaries ! We sighted 'em
Only this moment. By St. Nicholas
They must have sprung like Ghosts from underground,
Or, like the Devils they are, straight up from Hell.

ROBIN.

Crouch all into the bush !

[*The* FORESTERS *and* PEASANTS *hide behind the*
bushes.

MARIAN.

Take up the litter !

SIR RICHARD.

Move me no more ! I am sick and faint with pain !

MARIAN.

But, Sir, the Sheriff——

SIR RICHARD.

Let me be, I say !
The Sheriff will be welcome ! let me be !

MARIAN.

Give me my bow and arrows.   I remain
Beside my Father's litter.

ROBIN.

And fear not thou !
Each of us has an arrow on the cord ;
We all keep watch.

Enter SHERIFF OF NOTTINGHAM.

SHERIFF.

Marian !

MARIAN.

Speak not.   I wait upon a dying father.

SHERIFF.

The debt hath not been paid.   She will be mine.
What are you capering for ?   By old St. Vitus
Have you gone mad ?   Has it been paid ?

ABBOT (*dancing*).

O yes.

SHERIFF.

Have I lost her then?

JUSTICIARY (*dancing*).

     Lost her? O no, we took
Advantage of the letter—O Lord, the vein!
Not paid at York—the wood—prick me no more!

SHERIFF.

What pricks thee save it be thy conscience, man?

JUSTICIARY.

 By my halidome I felt him at my leg still. Where
be they gone to?

SHERIFF.

Thou art alone in the silence of the forest
Save for this maiden and thy brother Abbot,
And this old crazeling in the litter there.

Enter on one side FRIAR TUCK *from the bush, and on
  the other* PRINCE JOHN *and his* SPEARMEN, *with
  banners and trumpets, etc.*

JUSTICIARY (*examining his leg*).

They have missed the vein.

ABBOT.

And we shall keep the land.

SHERIFF.

Sweet Marian, by the letter of the law
It seems thy father's land is forfeited.

SIR RICHARD.

No! let me out of the litter.   He shall wed thee :
The land shall still be mine.   Child, thou shalt wed
    him,
Or thine old father will go mad—he will,
He will—he feels it in his head.

MARIAN.
                            O peace !
Father, I cannot marry till Richard comes.

SIR RICHARD.

And then the Sheriff !

MARIAN.

                    Ay, the Sheriff, father,
Would buy me for a thousand marks in gold—
Sell me again perchance for twice as much.
A woman's heart is but a little thing,
Much lighter than a thousand marks in gold ;

But pity for a father, it may be,
Is weightier than a thousand marks in gold.
I cannot love the Sheriff.

SIR RICHARD.

But thou wilt wed him?

MARIAN.

Ay, save King Richard, when he comes, forbid me.
Sweet heavens, I could wish that all the land
Were plunged beneath the waters of the sea,
Tho' all the world should go about in boats.

FRIAR TUCK.

Why, so should all the love-sick be sea-sick.

MARIAN.

Better than heart-sick, friar.

PRINCE JOHN (*to* SHERIFF).

See you not
They are jesting at us yonder, mocking us?
Carry her off, and let the old man die.
                    [*Advancing to* MARIAN.
Come, girl, thou shalt along with us on the instant.

FRIAR TUCK (*brandishing his staff*).

Then on the instant I will break thy head.

SHERIFF.

Back, thou fool-friar! Knowest thou not the Prince?

FRIAR TUCK (*muttering*).

He may be prince; he is not gentleman.

PRINCE JOHN.

Look! I will take the rope from off thy waist
And twist it round thy neck and hang thee by it.
Seize him and truss him up, and carry her off.

[FRIAR TUCK *slips into the bush.*

MARIAN (*drawing the bow*).

No nearer to me! back! My hand is firm,
Mine eye most true to one hair's-breadth of aim.
You, Prince, our king to come—you that dishonour
The daughters and the wives of your own faction—
Who hunger for the body, not the soul—
This gallant Prince would have me of his—what?
Household? or shall I call it by that new term
Brought from the sacred East, his harem? Never,
Tho' you should queen me over all the realms
Held by King Richard, could I stoop so low
As mate with one that holds no love is pure,
No friendship sacred, values neither man
Nor woman save as tools—God help the mark—
To his own unprincely ends. And you, you, Sheriff,

[*Turning to the* SHERIFF.

Who thought to buy your marrying me with gold,
Marriage is of the soul, not of the body.
Win me you cannot, murder me you may,
And all I love, Robin, and all his men,
For I am one with him and his ; but while
I breathe Heaven's air, and Heaven looks down on
    me,
And smiles at my best meanings, I remain
Mistress of mine own self and mine own soul

      [*Retreating, with bow drawn, to the bush.*
Robin !

ROBIN.

    I am here, my arrow on the cord.
He dies who dares to touch thee.

PRINCE JOHN.

               Advance, advance !
What, daunted by a garrulous, arrogant girl !
Seize her and carry her off into my castle.

SHERIFF.

Thy castle !

PRINCE JOHN.

    Said I not, I loved thee, man ?
Risk not the love I bear thee for a girl.

SHERIFF.

Thy castle !

PRINCE JOHN.

See thou thwart me not, thou fool !
When Richard comes he is soft enough to pardon
His brother ; but all those that held with him,
Except I plead for them, will hang as high
As Haman.

SHERIFF.

She is mine.   I have thy promise.

PRINCE JOHN.

O ay, she shall be thine—first mine, then thine,
For she shall spend her honeymoon with me.

SHERIFF.

Woe to that land shall own thee for her king !

PRINCE JOHN.

Advance, advance !

> [*They advance shouting.   The* KING *in
> armour reappears from the wood.*

KING RICHARD.

What shouts are these that ring along the wood ?

FRIAR TUCK (*coming forward*).

Hail, knight, and help us.   Here is one would clutch
Our pretty Marian for his paramour,
This other, willy-nilly, for his bride.

KING RICHARD.

Damsel, is this the truth?

MARIAN.

Ay, noble knight.

FRIAR TUCK.

Ay, and she will not marry till Richard come.

KING RICHARD (*raising his vizor*).

I am here, and I am he.

PRINCE JOHN (*lowering his, and whispering to his men*).

It is not he—his face—tho' very like—
No, no! we have certain news he died in prison.
Make at him, all of you, a traitor coming
In Richard's name—it is not he—not he.

[*The men stand amazed.*

FRIAR TUCK (*going back to the bush*).

Robin, shall we not move?

ROBIN.

It is the King
Who bears all down.   Let him alone awhile.
He loves the chivalry of his single arm.
Wait till he blow the horn.

FRIAR TUCK (*coming back*).

            If thou be king,
Be not a fool! Why blowest thou not the horn?

KING RICHARD.

I that have turn'd their Moslem crescent pale—
I blow the horn against this rascal rout!
    [FRIAR TUCK *plucks the horn from him and blows.*
       RICHARD *dashes alone against the* SHERIFF
       and JOHN'S *men, and is almost borne down,*
       when ROBIN *and his men rush in and rescue him.*

KING RICHARD (*to* ROBIN HOOD).

Thou hast saved my head at the peril of thine own.

PRINCE JOHN.

A horse! a horse! I must away at once;
I cannot meet his eyes. I go to Nottingham.
Sheriff, thou wilt find me at Nottingham.   [*Exit.*

SHERIFF.

If anywhere, I shall find thee in hell.
What! go to slay his brother, and make *me*
The monkey that should roast his chestnuts for him!

KING RICHARD.

I fear to ask who left us even now.

ROBIN.

I grieve to say it was thy father's son.
Shall I not after him and bring him back?

KING RICHARD.

No, let him be.   Sheriff of Nottingham,

[SHERIFF *kneels.*

I have been away from England all these years,
Heading the holy war against the Moslem,
While thou and others in our kingless realms
Were fighting underhand unholy wars
Against your lawful king.

SHERIFF.

My liege, Prince John—

KING RICHARD.

Say thou no word against my brother John.

SHERIFF.

Why then, my liege, I have no word to say.

KING RICHARD (*to* ROBIN).

My good friend Robin, Earl of Huntingdon,
For Earl thou art again, hast thou no fetters
For those of thine own band who would betray thee?

ROBIN.

I have ; but these were never worn as yet.
I never found one traitor in my band.

KING RICHARD.

Thou art happier than thy king.   Put him in chains.
                              [*They fetter the* SHERIFF.

ROBIN.

Look o'er these bonds, my liege.
          [*Shows the* KING *the bonds.   They talk together.*

KING RICHARD.

You, my lord Abbot, you Justiciary,
                    [*The* ABBOT *and* JUSTICIARY *kneel.*
I made you Abbot, you Justiciary :
You both are utter traitors to your king.

JUSTICIARY.

O my good liege, we did believe you dead.

ROBIN.

Was justice dead because the King was dead ?
Sir Richard paid his monies to the Abbot.
You crost him with a quibble of your law.

KING RICHARD.

But on the faith and honour of a king
The land is his again.

SIR RICHARD.

The land! the land!
I am crazed no longer, so I have the land.
[Comes out of the litter and kneels.
God save the King!

KING RICHARD (*raising* SIR RICHARD).

I thank thee, good Sir Richard.
Maid Marian.

MARIAN.

Yes, King Richard.

KING RICHARD.

Thou wouldst marry
This Sheriff when King Richard came again
Except—

MARIAN.

The King forbad it.   True, my liege.

KING RICHARD.

How if the King command it?

MARIAN.

Then, my liege,
If you would marry me with a traitor sheriff,
I fear I might prove traitor with the sheriff.

KING RICHARD.

But if the King forbid thy marrying
With Robin, our good Earl of Huntingdon.

MARIAN.

Then will I live for ever in the wild wood.

ROBIN (*coming forward*).
And I with thee.

KING RICHARD.

On nuts and acorns, ha !
Or the King's deer ? Earl, thou when we were hence
Hast broken all our Norman forest-laws,
And scruplest not to flaunt it to our face
That thou wilt break our forest laws again
When we are here.   Thou art overbold.

ROBIN.

My king,
I am but the echo of the lips of love.

L 2

KING RICHARD.

Thou hast risk'd thy life for mine : bind these two
    men.

[*They take the bags from the* ABBOT *and* JUSTICIARY,
        and proceed to fetter them.

JUSTICIARY.

But will the King, then, judge us all unheard ?
I can defend my cause against the traitors
Who fain would make me traitor.   If the King
Condemn us without trial, men will call him
An Eastern tyrant, not an English king.

ABBOT.

Besides, my liege, these men are outlaws, thieves,
They break thy forest laws—nay, by the rood
They have done far worse—they plunder—yea, ev'n
    bishops,
Yea, ev'n archbishops—if thou side with these,
Beware, O King, the vengeance of the Church.

FRIAR TUCK (*brandishing his staff*).

    I pray you, my liege, let me execute the vengeance
of the Church upon them.   I have a stout crabstick
here, which longs to break itself across their backs.

ROBIN.

Keep silence, bully friar, before the King.

FRIAR TUCK.

If a cat may look at a king, may not a friar speak
to one?

KING RICHARD.

I have had a year of prison-silence, Robin,
And heed him not—the vengeance of the Church!
Thou shalt pronounce the blessing of the Church
On those two here, Robin and Marian.

MARIAN.

He is but hedge-priest, Sir King.

KING RICHARD.

　　　　　　　　　And thou their Queen.
Our rebel Abbot then shall join your hands,
Or lose all hope of pardon from us—yet
Not now, not now—with after-dinner grace.
Nay, by the dragon of St. George, we shall
Do some injustice, if you hold us here
Longer from our own venison　　Where is it?
I scent it in the green leaves of the wood.

MARIAN.

First, king, a boon!

KING RICHARD.

　　　　　　Why surely ye are pardon'd,
Even this brawler of harsh truths—I trust

Half truths, good friar : ye shall with us to court.
Then, if ye cannot breathe but woodland air,
Thou Robin shalt be ranger of this forest,
And have thy fees, and break the law no more.

MARIAN.

It is not that, my lord.

KING RICHARD.

Then what, my lady ?

MARIAN.

This is the gala-day of thy return.
I pray thee, for the moment strike the bonds
From these three men, and let them dine with us,
And lie with us among the flowers, and drink—
Ay, whether it be gall or honey to 'em—
The king's good health in ale and Malvoisie.

KING RICHARD.

By Mahound I could dine with Beelzebub !
So now which way to the dinner ?

MARIAN.

Past the bank
Of foxglove, then to left by that one yew.
You see the darkness thro' the lighter leaf.
But look, who comes ?

Enter SAILOR.

SAILOR.

We heard Sir Richard Lea was here with Robin.
O good Sir Richard, I am like the man
In Holy Writ, who brought his talent back;
For tho' we touch'd at many pirate ports,
We ever fail'd to light upon thy son.
Here is thy gold again.　I am sorry for it.

SIR RICHARD.

The gold—my son—my gold, my son, the land—
Here Abbot, Sheriff—no—no, Robin Hood.

ROBIN.

Sir Richard, let that wait till we have dined.
Are all our guests here?

KING RICHARD.

　　　　　No—there's yet one other:
I will not dine without him.　Come from out
　　　　　　[*Enter* WALTER LEA.
That oak-tree!　This young warrior broke his prison
And join'd my banner in the Holy Land,
And cleft the Moslem turban at my side.
My masters, welcome gallant Walter Lea.
Kiss him, Sir Richard—kiss him, my sweet Marian.

MARIAN.

O Walter, Walter, is it thou indeed
Whose ransom was our ruin, whose return
Builds up our house again?   I fear I dream.
Here—give me one sharp pinch upon the cheek
That I may feel thou art no phantom—yet
Thou art tann'd almost beyond my knowing, brother.
                                        [*They embrace.*

WALTER LEA.

But thou art fair as ever, my sweet sister.

SIR RICHARD.

Art thou my son?

WALTER LEA.

I am, good father, I am.

SIR RICHARD.

I had despair'd of thee—that sent me crazed.
Thou art worth thy weight in all those marks of gold,
Yea, and the weight of the very land itself,
Down to the inmost centre.

ROBIN.

Walter Lea,

Give me that hand which fought for Richard there.
Embrace me, Marian, and thou, good Kate,

> [*To* KATE *entering.*

Kiss and congratulate me, my good Kate.

> [*She kisses him.*

LITTLE JOHN.

Lo now! lo now!
I have seen thee clasp and kiss a man indeed,
For our brave Robin is a man indeed.
Then by thine own account thou shouldst be mine.

KATE

Well then, who kisses first?

LITTLE JOHN.

> Kiss both together.
> [*They kiss each other.*

ROBIN.

Then all is well.   In this full tide of love,
Wave heralds wave : thy match shall follow mine (*to*
    LITTLE JOHN).
Would there were more—a hundred lovers more
To celebrate this advent of our King!
Our forest games are ended, our free life,
And we must hence to the King's court.   I trust

We shall return to the wood.   Meanwhile, farewell
Old friends, old patriarch oaks.   A thousand winters
Will strip you bare as death, a thousand summers
Robe you life-green again.   *You* seem, as it were,
Immortal, and we mortal.   How few Junes
Will heat our pulses quicker!   How few frosts
Will chill the hearts that beat for Robin Hood!

MARIAN.

And yet I think these oaks at dawn and even,
Or in the balmy breathings of the night,
Will whisper evermore of Robin Hood.
We leave but happy memories to the forest.
We dealt in the wild justice of the woods.
All those poor serfs whom we have served will bless
         us,
All those pale mouths which we have fed will praise
         us—
All widows we have holpen pray for us,
Our Lady's blessed shrines throughout the land
Be all the richer for us.   You, good friar,
You Much, you Scarlet, you dear Little John,
Your names will cling like ivy to the wood.
And here perhaps a hundred years away
Some hunter in day-dreams or half asleep
Will hear our arrows whizzing overhead,
And catch the winding of a phantom horn.

Robin.

And surely these old oaks will murmur thee
Marian along with Robin.   I am most happy—
Art thou not mine?—and happy that our King
Is here again, never I trust to roam
So far again, but dwell among his own.
Strike up a stave, my masters, all is well.

SONG WHILE THEY DANCE A COUNTRY DANCE.

Now the King is home again, and nevermore to roam
    again,
Now the King is home again, the King will have his
    own again,
Home again, home again, and each will have his own
    again,
All the birds in merry Sherwood sing and sing him
    home again.

THE END

Printed by R. & R. CLARK, *Edinburgh.*

Printed in Great Britain
by Amazon.co.uk, Ltd.,
Marston Gate.